WRITERS AND THEIR WORK

ISOBEL ARMSTRONG
General Editor

D1102900

REVENGE TRAGEDIES
OF
THE RENAISSANCE

The Spanish Tragedie:

OR,

Hieronimo is mad againe.

Containing the lamentable end of *Don Horatio*, and *Belimperia* ; with the pittifull death of *Hieronimo*.

Newly corrected, amended, and enlarged with new Additions of the *Painters* part, and others, as it hath of late been diuers times acted.

LONDON,
Printed by W. White, for I. White and T. Langley,
and are to be fold at their Shop ouer againft the
Sarazens head without New-gate. 1615.

Title page, *The Spanish Tragedy* (1615).
Reproduced with the permission of the British Library.

REVENGE TRAGEDIES
OF
THE RENAISSANCE

Janet Clare

In memory of Barbara Peters
and Inga-Stina Ewbank

© Copyright 2006 by Janet Clare

First published in 2006 by Northcote House Publishers Ltd, Horndon, Tavistock, Devon, PL19 9NQ, United Kingdom.
Tel: +44 (0) 1822 810066 Fax: +44 (0) 1822 810034.

British Library Cataloguing-in-Publication Data
A catalogue record for this book is available from the British Library

ISBN 0-7463-1085-4 hardcover
ISBN 0-7463-0918-X paperback

Typeset by PDQ Typesetting, Newcastle-under-Lyme
Printed and bound in the United Kingdom

Contents

Illustrations

Acknowledgements

I am very grateful to colleagues and friends who read sections of this book and were generous with their time and comments: Anne Fogarty, Frank McGuinness, Peter Culhane and, especially, Raymond Hargreaves. As always, I am indebted to John Gallagher for all his support and to the late Douglas Jefferson, who discussed some revenge plays with me in the book's early stages. Students in my 'Hamlet and Renaissance Revenge Tragedies' seminar at University College Dublin, particularly William Moore, Mary Boland, Kevin Power and Aoife Mahon, provided an invaluable forum for the development of some of the ideas in this book.

I would like to acknowledge the help I have had from Gavin Clarke of the Royal National Theatre Archive, from Susan Brock and Helen Hargest of the Shakespeare Centre, Stratford-upon-Avon, and from Janet Birkett of the Theatre Museum, Covent Garden. I am grateful to the Shakespeare Trust's Jubilee Education Fund for a generous grant towards the reproduction of photographs.

This book is dedicated to the memory of two wonderful teachers and academics. I first read and saw several of the plays discussed in this book while at school. Without the intellectual stimulation and academic encouragement of Barbara Peters it could not have been written. The lectures and work of Inga-Stina Ewbank as a scholar of Renaissance drama, and latterly her friendship, have been a source of continued inspiration.

Biographical and Historical Outline

The date of the first performance of many Renaissance plays can only be approximate. The year given is the earliest possible date as recorded in Alfred Harbage and S. Schoenbaum, *Annals of English Drama 975–1700*, third edition, revised by Sylvia Stoler Wagonheim (London, 1989).

DRAMATISTS

Thomas Kyd	born 1558, died 1594
Henry Chettle	born c.1560, died 1607
George Chapman	born c.1560, died 1634
William Shakespeare	born 1564, died 1616
Thomas Middleton	born 1570, died 1627
Thomas Heywood	born c.1570, died 1641
John Marston	born 1576, died 1634
John Fletcher	born 1579, died 1625
John Webster	born c.1580, died 1634
Francis Beaumont	born c.1584, died 1616
John Ford	born 1586, died post-1640

CHRONOLOGY

1562   Thomas Sackville and Thomas Norton, *Gorboduc* (Christmas revels at the Inner Temple).

1567   Construction of the first purpose-built theatre, the Red Lion, in Stepney, London.
       Translation by Arthur Golding of Ovid's *Metamorphoses*.

1561	Birth of Francis Bacon.
1569	Suppression of the Corpus Christi plays in York.
1576	Construction of the Theatre by James Burbage.
1581	Centralized system of theatrical censorship enforced under the Master of the Revels.
	Publication by Thomas Newton of *Seneca his Tenne Tragedies*.
1587	Construction of the Rose playhouse on the Bankside.
	Thomas Kyd, *The Spanish Tragedy* (performed in 1592 by Strange's Men). Play revised 1601–2.
	Execution of Mary Queen of Scots.
1588	The Spanish Armada.
	Thomas Hughes, *The Misfortunes of Arthur* (Gray's Inn at Court).
1589	A lost play of *Hamlet*, possibly by Thomas Kyd.
1589–92	William Shakespeare, probably with Pembroke's Men, composes his first plays.
1592–94	Re-grouping of theatrical companies; formation of Lord Chamberlain's Men (Shakespeare's Company) and the Admiral's Men (their chief rivals). Plays performed at the Theatre and the Rose.
1593	Death of Christopher Marlowe.
1594	Shakespeare, *Titus Andronicus* (?Pembroke's Men).
1597	Publication of Bacon's *Essays*, including 'Of Revenge'.
1599	Opening of the Globe.
	Revival of companies of boy actors.
	Certain verse satires, including work of John Marston, ordered to be publicly burnt.
	Shakespeare, *Julius Caesar* (Chamberlain's Men).
1600	John Marston, *Antonio's Revenge* (Children at Paul's).
	Shakespeare, *Hamlet* (Chamberlain's Men).
1601	Essex's rebellion. Execution of the Earl of Essex for treason.
1602	John Webster begins to write for the stage.
	Henry Chettle, *The Tragedy of Hoffman, or A Revenge for a Father* (Admiral's Men).
1603	Death of Queen Elizabeth. Accession of James I.
	Lord Chamberlain's Men become the King's Men.
	Publication of John Florio's translation of Montaigne's *Essays*.

1604   Patent granted to the company at the indoor theatre at Blackfriars: the Children of the Queen's Revels. Thomas Middleton begins to write satirical comedies of London life for the Children at Paul's.

1605   Gunpowder plot. Inigo Jones begins designing court masques. Thomas Middleton, *The Revenger's Tragedy* (King's Men).

1607   Thomas Heywood, *The Rape of Lucrece* (Queen Anne's).

1610   Francis Beaumont and John Fletcher, *The Maid's Tragedy* (King's Men). George Chapman, *The Revenge of Bussy D'Ambois* (Children of Whitefriars).

1611   Cyril Tourneur, *The Atheist's Tragedy or The Honest Man's Revenge* (?King's Men).

1612   John Webster, *The White Devil* (Queen Anne's).

1614   John Webster, *The Duchess of Malfi* (King's Men).

1615   John Ford, *'Tis Pity She's a Whore* (later performed by Queen Henrietta's Men).

1620   Thomas Middleton, *Women Beware Women* (? King's Men).

1622   Thomas Middleton and William Rowley, *The Changeling* (Lady Elizabeth's Men).

1625   Death of James I; accession of Charles I.

References and Abbreviations

I have quoted Shakespeare from the most recent Arden editions of the plays: *Titus Andronicus*, ed. Jonathan Bate (London, 1995); *Hamlet*, ed. Harold Jenkins (London, 1982).

Quotations from *The Spanish Tragedy*, *The Revenger's Tragedy*, *The Atheist's Tragedy* and *The Revenge of Bussy D'Ambois* are from *Four Revenge Tragedies*, ed. Katherine Eisaman Maus (Oxford, 1995).

Other citations are from the following editions of the plays:

Francis Beaumont and John Fletcher, *The Maid's Tragedy*, ed. T. W. Craik, Revels Plays (Manchester, 1988)

Henry Chettle, *The Tragedy of Hoffman*, ed. Harold Jenkins (Oxford, 1951)

John Ford, *'Tis Pity She's a Whore*, ed. Derek Roper, Revels Plays (London, 1975)

John Marston, *Antonio's Revenge*, ed. Reavley Gair, Revels Plays (Manchester, 1978)

Thomas Middleton, *Women Beware Women*, ed. J. R. Mulryne, Revels Plays (London, 1975)

Thomas Middleton and William Rowley, *The Changeling*, ed. N. W. Bawcutt, Revels Plays (London, 1958; reprinted with additions, 1961)

Thomas Sackville and Thomas Norton, *Gorboduc* in *Two Tudor Tragedies*, ed. William Tydeman (London, 1992)

Seneca, *Thyestes* in *Four Tragedies and Octavia*, trans. E. F. Watling (Harmondsworth, 1966)

John Webster, *The White Devil*, ed. John Russell Brown, Revels Plays (London, 1966)

John Webster, *The Duchess of Malfi*, ed. John Russell Brown, Revels Plays (London, 1964)

Biblical references are from the King James Bible (1611).

Abbreviations used in the notes:

PMLA *Publications of the Modern Language Association*
SEL *Studies in English Literature*

Introduction:
Revenge and Revenge Tragedy

Revenge, as the infliction of harm in righteous response to perceived injury or injustice, is a universal practice, transcultural and pan-historical. As is most often the case in tragedy, the enactment of revenge can be a personal desire, a sacred duty that falls upon a member of a family or clan; or it can be part of the collective consciousness of a victimized people. From duels to punishment beatings, the impulse to revenge is a primitive drive to retribution: A kills B and must be made to pay with his life by someone who identifies with B. Retributive justice is seen as effecting closure and restoring balance. Its starkest articulation within the Judeao-Christian tradition is to be found in Exodus: 'And if any mischief follow then thou shalt give life for life, eye for eye, tooth for tooth, hand for hand, foot for foot, burning for burning, wound for wound, stripe for stripe' (Exodus 21:23–5). In the shockingly spectacular theatre of Renaissance revenge tragedy we find the literal enactment of such forms of retaliation; an original act of bodily mutilation is replicated in a reprisal which matches or, more often, exceeds the offence.

Indeed, acts of revenge tend to be more cruel and insatiable than other acts of aggression. The very vocabulary of revenge, its constitutive metaphors, gives expression to this extreme punitive quality, as in the term 'thirst for revenge', and both the verbal and the visual imagery of revenge tragedies convey this compelling sense of thirst and appetite: 'Now could I drink hot blood,/ And do such bitter business as the day/ Would quake to look at' (III. ii. 351–3) declares Hamlet, sure now of the king's guilt, for once assuming the posture of a conventional avenger. There is a kind of grotesque appropriateness in equating

1

revenge with feasting, in terms of the metaphors and cognates of satiation. In *Titus Andronicus* Shakespeare borrows from the description in Seneca's *Thyestes* of Atreus's revenge on his brother Thyestes in depicting the repayment of atrocity as culminating in the spectacularly brutal form of the cannibalistic feast. A similar literal working of the vengeful appetite is represented in John Marston's *Antonio's Revenge* when Antonio determines that his antagonist Piero will 'feed on life', in this case Piero's innocent son Julio. Antonio goes only so far as to present Piero with a dish containing his son's limbs, but his barely submerged desire to close vengeance with a cannibalistic banquet is clear. In Thomas Kyd's *The Spanish Tragedy* Hieronimo imagines a fate for his son's murderers which stops just short of devouring them: he will, he declares, appeal to Proserpine in the underworld that she 'may grant/ Revenge on them that murdered my son/ Then will I rend and tear them thus and thus,/ Shivering their limbs in pieces with my teeth' (III. xiii. 120–3). In *Titus Andronicus* and *Antonio's Revenge* the respective appetites of the revenger and of the offender ironically coalesce: the metaphorical appetite of revenge is satisfied by the spectacle or anticipation of the enemy's physical satiation.

Seen from a social and moral perspective, such real or imaginatively projected acts, evoking excesses of cruelty, would be judged grotesque and deplorable and revenge the unleashing of a base and dangerous emotion. Certainly, revenge is commonly regarded as a barbaric practice because of its violent extremes which frequently exceed an 'eye for an eye', perpetuating indiscriminate and often gratuitous killing. Yet, the response evoked by some revenge tragedies is more ambivalent as we witness or hear of an injury – often cold-blooded murder – that is itself base and dangerous and causes the protagonist to experience gross injustice and an unbearable sense of loss. From the perspective of a suffering individual, revenge can be representative of a morally considered desire to keep faith with the dead and a ritual of closure that brings liberation for the protagonist. But it can extend beyond this, in that revenge may be represented as conceivably the only way of restoring order in a society where the political and moral framework has been violated. The original offence is so great that nothing less than extreme, counterbalancing wounds can be inflicted.

The ambivalence of feeling aroused by the misery of the wronged individual or individuals, on the one hand, and the wreckage of revenge on the other, has made revenge a compelling dramatic form. Moreover, the extremity of the emotions released in such acts, as well as the spectacular closure they induce, has made revenge a recurrent subject of national drama. From the Greek tragedies of Aeschylus, Sophocles and Euripides, whose myths were adapted, stripped of some of their dignity, by the Roman philosopher and dramatist Seneca, through to revenge and honour in Golden Age Spanish drama of Lope de Vega and Calderón and their contemporaries of the English Renaissance, revenge is a dramatic form with an extensive cultural history. Dramatists have understood how grief turns to anger so that the desire to revenge becomes a violent obsession and, equally, the visceral fascination this creates as theatre. Loss and rage distort the psyche of the revenger and a determination is forged that retaliation should exceed the original offence. In *The Spanish Tragedy*, generally regarded as the first revenge play of the Elizabethan commercial, popular theatres, Hieronimo resolves to revenge the murder of his son Horatio by Lorenzo, the nephew of the King of Spain; but he also vows that the killing will not stop with Lorenzo. He declares that he will 'marshal up the fiends in hell/ To be revenged on you all for this' (III. xii. 77–8). 'You all', in the play's catastrophe, includes the prince's innocent father, the Duke of Castile, so that in the final reckoning the Spanish line of succession is wiped out. In feuds – real or fictional – vengeance breeds vengeance; violence escalates and all parties are consumed in a domino effect of hatred and retaliation.

The prime motivation for such atrocious acts is the emotion of anger which moral philosophers such as Plato, Seneca and Cicero, widely read in the Renaissance, had argued was better to be eradicated altogether while recognizing its deep-rooted nature. Concluding his essay on anger, Montaigne quotes Aristotle's observation that choler can serve 'virtue and valour as a weapon'; but, adds Montaigne, 'it must be some new-fangled weapon; for we wield the other weapons: that one wields us; it is not our hand that guides it: it guides our hand; it gets a hold on us: not we on it.'[1] Seneca, in three moral essays describing anger as the most terrible and frenzied of all the

3

emotions, advocated the Stoic remedy of restraint.[2] Seneca's plays of revenge – rhetorical dramas of declaration, not performance – show the ghastly effects of anger. Figures such as Hecuba, Medea, Atreus and Hercules are overwhelmed by it and subsequently enact the most hideous forms of vengeance. Thyestes murders his brother's children; Medea murders her own children in revenge against her adulterous husband Jason; and Phaedre plots the destruction of her stepson Hippolytus when he is unresponsive to her desires. The emotional dynamics of revenge cause the abandonment of restraint and can produce psychic disorder. In plays of the Renaissance we witness protagonists like Titus in *Titus Andronicus* and Hieronimo in *The Spanish Tragedy* metamorphosed by anger, devising and performing atrocities. Anger feeds on anger and in both these figures leads to moments of mental breakdown and insanity.

In his often-quoted essay 'On Revenge', Francis Bacon differentiated between public revenge, an example of which he gave as the death of Caesar and which is 'for the most part fortunate', and private revengers deemed mischievous, vindictive and unfortunate.[3] The suggestion is that if the pursuit of revenge is open and declared, rather than covert, the offence may be mitigated. It was the plotting of private revenge, often in the secluded setting of the court, which preoccupied Kyd, Shakespeare, Marston and Webster. Playwrights, however, invest revenge with varied moral shading according to the nature of the private revenger. On the one hand, we have revengers who act, as they see it, to bring justice and restore balance; on the other, there are characters who declare revenge and act in ways that are destructively self-advancing. Extreme figures of hatred like Lorenzo in *The Spanish Tragedy*, Iago in *Othello* and Aaron in *Titus Andronicus* appropriate or usurp revenge as their motive while Titus, Hieronimo and Hamlet associate revenge with justice and duty. Somewhere in between are figures like Vindici in *The Revenger's Tragedy* and Bosola in *The Duchess of Malfi*.

As is clear from its usage in non-dramatic texts of the period, revenge was not exclusively imbricated with issues of justice, but also stemmed from less elevated instincts. John Norden, in *The Mirror of Honour*, for example, commenting on the essential qualities of the military commander, warns against envy, 'for it

4

feedeth only upon the damnable desires of doing injury in the best' and a marginal note is added, 'Envy will find matter to bear colour of lawful revenge'.[4] In juxtaposing 'lawful' and 'revenge', it is accepted that revenge may in some circumstances be justified, while the point remains that, in Norden's observation, revenge is used falsely to represent acts dictated by sinister motives. There are illustrations of this appropriation in the plays discussed in this book, as we see characters, identified in Freudian terms as all id and ego, and bent on nothing but self-advancement, employing the term revenge simply to remove those who obstruct their desires.

If the revenger is far from a type character, what distinguishes one forced by circumstance to plot in secret for some kind of just reprisal from a villain who may deploy the term revenge as a rationale for deadly intrigue? One possible distinction is that with the latter there is an opacity of motive. Further, the spurious revenger continues to shroud his action in secrecy once the deed is done, while the revenger obsessed with obtaining some kind of justice lays claim to his act. Lorenzo in *The Spanish Tragedy*, after the murder of Horatio further conspires to cover his tracks and wants his part to remain forever unknown. Iago's last contemptuous words are 'Demand me nothing. What you know, you know./ From this time forth I never will speak word.' On the other hand, at the close of *The Revenger's Tragedy* Vindici proudly and – consistent with the play's tone – gleefully acknowledges himself and his brother as the duke's murderers: 'We may be bold/ To speak it now. 'Twas somewhat witty carried,/ Though we say it; 'twas we two murdered him' (V. iii. 95–7). The admission leads to his own execution. Hamlet's dying words are a request to his friend Horatio to report his 'cause aright' and 'tell his story'. For the protagonist of revenge plays the act of revenge is one of closure, figuratively and literally as, in his public identification with his deed, reparation is made for the past and is sealed with his own death, while the malicious schemer dies taking his secrets to the grave.

For the moralist such distinctions in the twisted or in the psychologically complex motivations of revenge are largely irrelevant. In Bacon's view society cannot function if individuals are allowed to seek redress on their own: 'The more man's nature runs to [revenge], the more ought law to weed it out.' A system of justice can be seen as a human best endeavour to provide an objective and impartial means of redressing wrongs. A criminal justice system imposing formal punishment also externalizes grief and offers the would-be avenger satisfaction. Yet what happens when the offender is the sovereign or head of state as, for example, in *Hamlet*, *Antonio's Revenge*, *The Maid's Tragedy* and *The Revenger's Tragedy*, or when justice is unobtainable, as in *The Spanish Tragedy* and *Titus Andronicus*? Bacon acknowledges that 'the most tolerable sort of revenge is for those wrongs for which there is no remedy', but with the caveat 'Let a man take heed the revenge be such as there is no law to punish; else a man's enemy is still beforehand, and it is two for one.' The corrupt state where wrongs cannot be remedied is a recurring location for Renaissance plays as well as a metaphor, as in *Hamlet*, for a more endemic human corruption. Where there is no legal redress, an unwritten code is invoked. Revenge does not necessarily put the law out of office, as Bacon affirms it does, because in plays like *The Spanish Tragedy*, *Antonio's Revenge* and *The Duchess of Malfi* the law is seen to have no office in the first place. Then the code of revenge becomes the closest approximation to law: a rough justice, or, as Bacon declared, a 'wild justice', on the brink of anarchy.

There is no evidence in English Renaissance culture that revenge was or could ever be officially condoned.[5] For the legislator revenge was repugnant to the natural law, while for the moralist it was considered barbaric. In 1612 a Scottish noble Lord Sanquire was brought to trial for taking vengeance on a man who several years earlier had blinded him in one eye in a fencing match.[6] Francis Bacon, as Solicitor General, equated the crime with vengeance: 'Your temptation was revenge, which the more natural it is to man, the more have laws, both divine and human, sought to repress it.' Bacon couples social and religious prohibition. Yet biblical teaching was tangled and sometimes paradoxical. On the one hand, as has been noted, the vengeful god of Exodus, almost adumbrating the retributive bodily mutilations of Renaissance tragedy, advocates 'eye for eye, tooth for tooth'. Again, in Numbers God tells Moses, 'The revenger of blood himself shall slay the murderer: when he meeteth him, he shall slay him' (35:19). In Psalms there is exultation in revenge: 'The righteous shall rejoice when he seeth the vengeance: he shall wash his feet in the blood of the wicked' (58:10). But this approval of violent retribution is superseded by the teaching of the New Testament where the would-be revenger finds little support for his actions. St Paul in his letter to the Ephesians exhorts 'Be ye angry, and sin not: let not the sun go down upon your wrath' (4:26). Paul makes it explicit that vengeance usurps divine prerogative: 'Recompense to no man evil for evil' (Romans, 12:17) and adds the much cited clause, 'Avenge not yourselves, but rather give place unto wrath: for it is written, Vengeance is mine; I will repay, saith the Lord' (Romans, 12:19). The avenger might, however, see a loophole here; just as Hamlet reflects on himself as God's 'scourge and minister' (III. iv. 176), the revenger might fashion himself as an agent of divine justice or chastisement. But, overall, armed with New Testament scripture, the theologian could only condemn revenge, and the revenger has to quote selectively to find any biblical sanction for his actions.

We cannot, though, innocently adopt dominant Elizabethan ideologies against revenge as the context for reading revenge tragedy. As an aesthetic domain, theatre is not bound to replicate its culture's orthodoxy. The instincts and dilemmas which inhere in revenge, resisted in Bacon's essay, make for powerful theatre as the dramatist explores what the law-giver forbids as an individual enterprise. In plays of revenge the revenger is humanized, his predicament individualized and, through the theatrical convention of the soliloquy, the audience has access to the recesses of his mind. Moreover, by showing the avenger's inner self in conflict with the corrupt political world he inhabits, the playwright can problematize the official morality of revenge. There is a touch of the rebel or revolutionary in several avengers in Renaissance theatre, as they rise up against a state of the world they find intolerable. Certainly, in drama stretching over several decades from the 1580s onwards, questions are raised which are largely absent in anti-revenge advocacy. How does a protagonist respond to a situation where revenge must be taken against a tyrant ruler, even though it remains treason and means almost certain death for the avenger? What happens when revenge is expected of an individual not necessarily predisposed to act in such a way, as in *Hamlet*? What happens psychologically to the individual in the process of becoming a revenger? Bacon does indeed hint at a response when he claims at the end of his essay that 'vindictive people live the life of witches'; but only the drama can represent the terrible pressures on the mind created by the obligation to revenge. Within the often extravagant and discursive plotting of the revenge plays of the Renaissance such issues are embedded.

While these tragedies of revenge engage the audience at moral, psychological, emotional and political levels, arguably their most immediate impact lies in the ritualistic and spectacular quality they possess. The staging of the rituals of revenge is often visually impressive in symbolism and tableaux. In *Hoffman, Antonio's Revenge, The Revenger's Tragedy* and *'Tis Pity She's a Whore*, characters variously gather together to swear and then enact vengeance. Revenge tragedy is a theatre of cruelty and a theatre of blood, so much so that a play like *Titus Andronicus* with its human sacrifice, rape and mutilation and final act of cannibalism was judged so hideous that throughout the eighteenth century it was thought not to be Shakespeare's work.[7] But the play is of its kind. Whatever their exploration of ethical and political issues, revenge tragedies are visceral in their displays of horror and violence. Unlike the extreme acts of classical tragedy, Renaissance playwrights did not report the atrocity, but represented it on the stage. Audiences brought to the theatre not only prior theatrical experiences of revenge but other cultural and social associations. The ritualized 'justice' of the private avenger could be said to correspond to the theatre of punishment orchestrated by the state, which was witnessed by theatre audiences in the public execution. Revenge tragedies invert the process of state punishment and depict the subject acting violently against autocracy. In Henry Chettle's *Tragedy of Hoffman*, for example, the opening stage direction reads *strikes open a curtain where appears a body*. This is the corpse of Hoffman's father, executed by order of the state as a pirate and condemned to die by being crowned with a scorching hot crown. Hoffman addresses the corpse, 'the dead remembrance of my living father', and vows revenge. In the next scene he is represented as torturing to death with a searing crown his first victim, Prince Otho, thus replicating his father's death. The play closes with Hoffman about to meet the same fate as his father and Otho at the order of the Duke of Saxony. Here state revenge or punishment and private revenge or retaliation become mirror images of each other.

State punishment, like private revenge, was the rite that concluded the crime and exceeded the savagery of the crime itself.[8] The punishment of a traitor – the monarch's revenge – was the most horrendous of deaths: although a few were granted late reprieve, alleged traitors were drawn to the gallows, hung, disembowelled while still alive and then beheaded; aristocratic traitors were merely beheaded. As a symbol of the state's power to root out treason, the head of the traitor was displayed on Tower Bridge. The 'private' revenges of Antonio, Titus and Vindici are no more horrendous in their physical torment and in the triumphant acknowledgement of their vengeful acts than the institutionalized revenge of the scaffold. Public executions often bore the specific mark of the crime: the tongues of blasphemers were pierced; the right hand of a murderer was cut off. Such theatrical representation of the crime was in turn reproduced in the public theatres as revengers such as Hoffman, Hamlet, to a point, and Vindici imitate, in their acts of crowning and poisoning, the original 'offence' and employ a similar symbolism. In this sense, in the visual imagery they deploy, the plays do indeed re-present their culture's orthodoxy.

REVENGE AND GENRE

The appeal of revenge to playwrights both technically and aesthetically is obvious. In *Rosencrantz and Guildenstern are Dead* (1967), Tom Stoppard's inventive and metadramatic response to *Hamlet*, the Player remarks to Guildenstern, 'There's a design at work in all art – surely you know that? Events must play themselves out to aesthetic, moral and logical conclusion.'[9] Despite a certain flippancy, we can see how pertinent the observation is to revenge, which may be considered the dramatist's ideal weapon of choice, providing, as it does, a hand chain of cause and effect on which to play. As a catalyst for action, and as dramatic resolution, revenge, bound up with ideologies of tyranny and absolutism and with more domestic concerns of rivalry, love and honour, is remarkably adaptable to different kinds of drama. In time, the repetition of the theme and of accompanying motifs was to lead to elements of parody in plays like *The Revenger's Tragedy* and *Antonio's Revenge* or, as in *Hamlet*, more subtle and distinctive explorations of the complexities of revenge. This very resilience and flexibility of revenge as cause and motivation are demonstrated in the way that for decades, through to the mid seventeenth century, dramatists returned to and reshaped stories of revenge.[10]

Revenge – or the pursuit of revenge – is not, of course, exclusive to tragedy. In the Elizabethan history play, dynasties, factions and clans strive to avenge atrocities committed against them. Shakespeare's first tetralogy of history plays – the three *Henry VI* plays and *Richard III* – is structured on an extensive pattern of revenge as the Yorkists and Lancastrians kill in serial retaliation. In *Richard III* the balance which revenge is seen to effect is present in the play's rhetorical patterning, notably in the lines of the lamenting women. Queen Margaret in her rebuke to the Duchess of York bitterly reflects on their respective losses and the counterbalancing retribution: 'Thy Edward, he is dead, that killed my Edward:/ Thy other Edward dead, to quit my Edward;/ . . .Thy Clarence, he is dead, that stabbed my Edward' (IV. iv. 63–7). Revenge forms part of the epic scope of pre-Tudor history and as such it is represented less in terms of individual responsibility and compulsion and more in terms of historical necessity. This is less the case with Shakespeare's *Julius Caesar*, a classical history play that is structured on revenge. In deeming public revenge admissible, Bacon had cited the example of the assassination of Julius Caesar or rather the reprisal against the assassins. In *Julius Caesar*, however, no such clear moral exemplum emerges as we see the shaping of source material for theatrical purposes and its redirection for different political ends. Shakespeare invests the historical narrative with an element of the popular revenge play as Caesar's ghost appears to Brutus predicting the victory of Antony and Octavius over Brutus and Cassius at Philippi. The dramatic narrative is altogether more morally complex than Bacon's passing remark would seem to allow as the assassin Brutus considers that in murdering Caesar he is striking against tyranny. Mark Antony and Octavius act decisively, but clearly from mixed motives, to avenge the assassination. The play closes not with a sense of retribution and appeasement for the murder of Caesar, or the vindication of public revenge, but with a sense of loss at the death of Brutus, recognized by his opponents as a noble Roman. Interestingly, the dynamics of this historical revenge play contrast with those of fictive, popular revenge tragedy. In the latter, the audience often reaches some understanding of the loss and predicament of the avenger, whereas revenge in the history play is seen as a weapon consciously manipulated for political ascendancy.

As a universal response, revenge lends itself easily to comedy where it provides a way of settling scores, by bringing discomfiture and humiliation to the opponent, though not physical injury.[11] We can see this pattern in Marston's *The Malcontent* when the villain Mendoza is exposed and the restored Duke orders him literally to be kicked out of Genoa. In comedy, as so horrifically and spectacularly happens in tragedy, one act of retaliation begets another. In *Twelfth Night*, for example, a group of roisterers led by Sir Toby Belch take revenge on the puritanical steward Malvolio for suppressing their drunken revels by tricking him into believing that the mistress of the household is in love with him. Malvolio's subsequent humiliation and torment lead to a darkening of the mood of the comedy encapsulated in the threat to his tormentors of further retaliation in his exit line: 'I'll be revenged on the whole pack of you.' By its very nature revenge adds shades of darkness to comedy. One of the clearest illustrations of this is *The Merchant of Venice*, the most intractable of Shakespeare's so-called romantic comedies. There is an interesting fusion in this play of what in tragedy remains discrete; that is, private revenge which is identified with the institutionalized revenge of the law. In demanding a pound of Antonio's flesh as forfeiture for the merchant's failure to repay the loan, and in refusing Bassanio's offer of its double repayment, Shylock is clearly out for blood revenge. As Shylock *'whets his knife'* ready to slice Antonio's flesh thereby causing his death, and as Gratiano refers to the Jew's 'wolvish, bloody, starved, and ravenous' desires, we have the verbal and visual imagery of revenge tragedy. The difference here, of course, is that this is taking place in the civilized venue of the Venetian court presided over by the Duke.

11

Shylock embodies the spirit of revenge and yet operates within the parameters of the law and speaks the language of public justice. When Bassanio asks him 'Do all men kill the things they do not love?', Shylock's reply is animated by hatred for the Christian community (a hatred which can be understood within the play) and by thoughts of revenge, 'Hates any man the thing he would not kill?' Yet, as he reiterates, he stands for law, and Portia, disguised as the lawyer, accepts that, despite the strangeness of his case, the Venetian law cannot deny him. In his pursuit of private revenge pursued in public, Shylock is defeated not by Portia's eloquent disquisition on mercy, but, finally, by the law that is applied against him with the same literalism with which he invoked it. He is within his rights to demand a pound of Antonio's flesh, but not to spill one drop of Antonio's blood. Recognizing his defeat, Shylock is prepared to withdraw his demands and accept the money, but, here, refracting the perpetuating tendencies of revenge, Shylock is punished and humiliated by the court and the Christian community as he is forced to surrender his wealth and religion for threatening the life of a gentile. *The Merchant of Venice* just keeps within the bounds of comedy, but, in its depiction of revenge as colouring the relationship between Jew and Christian, there is a disturbing anatomization of the malice, envy and hatred that lie behind the supposed Venetian civility.

If genres other than tragedy employ motives and motifs of revenge, it can also be said that a strain of black comedy is intrinsic to revenge tragedy. Revenge tragedy is an unstable genre shot through with elements of the grotesque and liable to tilt into farce. Within the narrative structure of revenge plays and the excesses of retaliation there is a darkly comic potential. Taking the cue from Senecan avengers like Atreus, who declares 'You cannot say you have avenged a crime/ Unless you better it' (*Thyestes*, Act II, ll. 195–6), the retaliatory act outdoes the original crime. But there is often something so melodramatic in this very inordinate re-action that the audience, in some sense on the side of the revenger, may be provoked into uneasy laughter at his lavish, cruelly refined, but often aesthetically appropriate, contrivances. Grotesque action threatens to topple over into sickening farce, as in the cannibalistic feast in *Titus Andronicus* and, in *The Revenger's Tragedy*, Vindici's whetting of the Duke's

12

sexual desires with the dressed-up skeletal frame of Vindici's sometime lover Gloriana, before the Duke dies by kissing the poisoned skull. Laughter is a mechanism of release not only for the audience, but also for the characters, burdened with the task of revenge, who take refuge in hollow laughter. One of the defining moments in *Titus Andronicus* is when Titus hears that his sons, whom he thinks he has saved by lopping off his hand, have been executed: he can only laugh; he cannot even begin to grieve. Hamlet's bitter, sardonic humour, his quips and self-mockery may be seen as ways of articulating and rising above the conflicting pressures bearing down on him.

In his comprehensive study of revenge tragedy John Kerrigan has commented on the comic strain of the plays and distinguishes between the comic interludes and surprises of other tragedies, which criticism tends to integrate, and comic components of revenge plays, which spring spontaneously from tragic action. 'Repeatedly', concludes Kerrigan, 'vengeance generates from out of its dramaturgical potential a strain of awkward comedy which raises laughter and kills it.'[12] We could take this further and say that writers of revenge plays are conscious and highly manipulative of the comic strain which inheres in their material. For example, as Evadne, the female avenger of *The Maid's Tragedy*, ties the king to the bed ready to stab him to death, the king is made to exclaim to his lover, 'What pretty new device is this, Evadne?' (V. i. 47). Nervous laughter is thus released immediate to the heinous act of killing the king – a deed from which male characters have shied away. The enactment of revenge within a masque or play, as in *The Revenger's Tragedy*, *The Spanish Tragedy* and *Women Beware Women*, could be seen as something of a stage cliché, but again the aesthetic distancing associates revenge with 'play' and artifice, a contrived act which entertains as much as it disturbs or shocks. In such scenes there is considerable dramatic irony as we move between two levels of action – the apparent and the actual – and the semblance of the 'play' is revealed to a startled on-stage audience to be the murderous 'reality'.

Renaissance revenge tragedies, as this study will illustrate, are often highly metatheatrical in that playwrights borrowed visual and verbal images from earlier plays to enhance a theatrical artifice. At a time when originality was not particu-

13

larly valued, some recall of motifs in plays representing revenge is to be expected. Presumably, the spectators' pleasure in watching such plays was bound up with the recognition of redeployed devices they had witnessed in other works. In our own time, of all revenge plays, *Hamlet* has acquired a cultural centrality; but the textual evidence suggests this was true also in the early seventeenth century. In *The Atheist's Tragedy*, for example, Charlemont's meditations in the graveyard would surely have recalled Hamlet's evocative words as he gazes at the skull of Yorick, his father's jester, while the gravediggers are preparing the grave of Ophelia. The actual and the assumed madness in Chettle's *Hoffman* also betrays the influence of *Hamlet*. *The Spanish Tragedy* exerted its influence for decades on subsequent revenge plays, notably in depicting revenge as taking place under cover of a court entertainment or masque. Several revengers carry with them physical emblems, reminders of loss and duty: Hamlet writes down in his 'tables' the injunction of the ghost to kill Claudius; Vindici carries the skull of his dead lover Gloriana, and Hieronimo clasps the napkin stained with the blood of his son Horatio.

The formal features outlined above bring a certain coherence to a group of plays recognized as belonging to the tradition of revenge tragedy. From the early twentieth century it has been a critical practice to think of Renaissance plays with a revenge theme, modelled on Kyd's *The Spanish Tragedy* and displaying a debt to Seneca, as having a distinct generic identity.[13] In *Elizabethan Revenge Tragedy* Fredson Bowers examined the genealogy of revenge tragedy beginning with Kyd.[14] In Bowers's account the genre developed by incorporating Germanic and later Italian influences manifest in Jacobean and Caroline plays. A similar approach is reflected in a more recent study by Charles A. and Elaine S. Hallet, *The Revenger's Madness*, in which it is supposed that there is a certain configuration of formal elements – notably the appearance of a ghost and the madness, real or feigned, of the avenger – which defines and delimits the approach.[15] In her edition *Four Revenge Tragedies* Katherine Eisaman Maus finds more socio-political than dramatic congruence between plays as diverse as *The Revenger's Tragedy* and *The Revenge of Bussy D'Ambois* (the latter, with *The Atheist's Tragedy*, classified as an anti-revenge play). Maus acknowledges conventions and characteristics in common, however idiosyncratically they are displayed, and observes that a play of revenge can be better understood if it can be shown how it deviates from the norms of its genre.[16] What remains problematic is defining the norms of the genre other than in very general terms. Katherine Maus singles out the revenger's dilemma and his demands for justice in a politically corrupt world, rather than any shared dramatic or theatrical qualities. But, again, amongst the plays discussed in this study there is much variation in the motivations and actions of individual revengers and a demand for justice is not always paramount.

Formal elements can only roughly define a generic category: ghosts appear and characters go mad in plays other than revenge plays. Renaissance revenge plays, unlike classical antecedents constructed entirely upon an archetypal pattern of revenge orchestrated by the gods, are discursive in their action and despite some shared features each has its own peculiar accent in style and tone as well as its individual take on revenge. Few plays then can be said to concentrate entirely on, or expose, a fixed drive to revenge; typically, revenge plots become complicated by court politics and intrigue, and by love and sexual desire as well as counter-plots against the revenger. The need to revenge can be induced by a gross miscarriage of justice, but, equally, it is represented as a crime of passionate retaliation for an offence or slight and as such elicits quite different audience responses. Indeed, in later revenge plays honour, variously defined and sometimes quite cynically constructed, displaces justice as motivation. It is doubtful whether Renaissance dramatists were aware that they were consciously employing conventions of a defined tragic subgenre; few Renaissance plays in their titles or title pages, in which it was common practice to offer an elaborately descriptive subtitle, call attention to the revenge theme or to the role of the protagonist as revenger. Genres are not passively inherited, but made and re-made every time a new play is written and performed. Verbal or structural evocation of one revenge play does not necessarily indicate a consciousness of genre and tradition; it can also denote opportunistic borrowing. Indeed, the deployment of common motifs often highlights aesthetic difference rather than dependence.

The term 'revenge tragedy', with its implication of a specific subgenre of tragedy, is then in the main resisted in this study, as is the notion that *The Spanish Tragedy* can be regarded as a template for subsequent plays. As I have argued, the nature of revenge as it defines dramatic action is *per se* problematic. In *The Duchess of Malfi*, for example, there is a counterpointing of psychotic Ferdinand's perverted revenge against his widow sister, 'guilty' only in so far as she disobeys him in remarrying, with that of the intelligencer and murderer Bosola, whose conscience is awakened, and who caps his many roles by assuming that of the Duchess's revenger. Revenge was used to signify cultural 'otherness'. Marston in *Antonio's Revenge*, Middleton in *The Revenger's Tragedy* and *Women Beware Women* and Webster in *The White Devil* and *The Duchess of Malfi* exploited and heightened a perception of the Italian city states, with their counter-reformation ideologies, as locations of corruption, feud and blood revenge. When revenge can be associated with resentment as in Marston's *Antonio's Revenge* and Massinger's *Duke of Milan*, with a primitive and anarchic justice as in *Titus Andronicus* and *The Spanish Tragedy*, with providential justice as in *The Atheist's Tragedy* and with masculinity as in *The Revenge of Bussy D'Ambois*, the problems of establishing the genre become apparent.

With revenge so evident a theme in Renaissance drama, it is legitimate to ask why particular plays have been selected for discussion. The chapters will focus on plays in which revenge figures either as a motive of dramatic action, usually leading to the death of the protagonist, or as the matrix for more discursive dramatic action. Rather than group plays entirely in chronological order, the choice of texts discussed in individual chapters has largely been determined by shared dramatic concerns or by what revenge signifies in terms of justice, honour, divine vengeance, gender and national identity. It is, of course, necessary to have some sense of the dramatic chronology of revenge tragedies, if only to be aware of the antecedents of a specific play. But there is no simple trajectory of revenge tragedy to suggest that as it developed self-consciously, the form became, morally and aesthetically, outworn and decadent. There were parodies of revenge by Marston and Middleton in the early seventeenth century, implying a theatrical self-awareness, yet, years after such serio-comic representation, revenge was again presented with an ethical seriousness and psychological intensity. Some plays we will examine might seem only coincidentally revenge plays. While noting certain formal characteristics and evident debts and intertexts, the aim of this study will be, however, to consider each play on its own terms, examining both the configuration of revenge and the distinctive theatrical idiom.

Far from belonging to a genre that rehearses convention, revenge plays show themselves to be unpredictable in their ways of projecting ethical dilemma and unstable in their recourse to farce, satire, parody and melodrama. Bacon's axiom that revenge is a kind of wild justice is an oxymoron in so far as it implies the reparation of wrong through unruly and violent acts. 'Wild' also encapsulates something of the aesthetic experience of plays of revenge. Revengers, of course, become wild – distracted, demented, out of their wits, passionately vehement or impetuous. Similarly, the action itself is not easily controlled, as wild and spectacular responses bring us close to melodrama and laughter becomes a defence against the bleak experience of loss and violence. The wild justice we see enacted in these plays is a response to something we could, by analogy, describe as wild injustice. Its exponents, with their egotistical contempt for the lives of others, inhabit a menacing space of infantile wilfulness informed by adult urges. Theirs is a strange world, close to our worst fears and hidden desires, and this explains the sense of horror and fascination these plays continue to exert: a horror which is, of course, held in check by the various transformations effected by the illusion of theatre.

1

Revenge and Justice: Elizabethan Revenge Tragedies

The immense popularity of the first surviving revenge play of the newly established commercial theatre, Thomas Kyd's *The Spanish Tragedy*, spawned a dramatic preoccupation with the theme for several decades. Kyd, like Shakespeare, was not university educated, but the classical training he received at the Merchant Taylors' School in London is well demonstrated in the language, rhetorical style and imagery of *The Spanish Tragedy*. The financially precarious profession of playwright was one of the options available to a man with literary aspirations. Kyd's career followed a very different path from that of Shakespeare – he died in penury – but he made his mark as a pioneering dramatist for the newly established commercial theatre.[1] Indeed one critic has gone as far as to identify Kyd alongside Christopher Marlowe with the creation of Elizabethan tragedy.[2]

The intricate plotting, characterization and intuition of theatrical effect make Kyd's play highly original, although, like other popular revenge plays, it has antecedents in the academic drama, specifically the dramatic works of Seneca (c.4 BC–AD 65) and neo-Senecan drama. The plays of Seneca had been translated into English by Jasper Heywood, John Neville and John Studley in the mid sixteenth century and all the tragedies were published by Thomas Newton in 1581.[3] Seneca is often perceived solely in terms of the atrocious crimes which his plays relate and in this context *Thyestes* is most often cited as a prime example of a play dominated by the outrageous acts of a bloodthirsty revenger. In the play, Atreus, brother of Thyestes, is caught up in a cycle of revenge incited by Tantalus, his uncle,

18

whose tormented ghost summoned from the underworld appears at the beginning of the play, asking 'What ill am I appointed for?' In response to Thyestes's rape of his wife, Atreus plots to afflict him 'with greater pain'. A servant comments incredulously on Atreus's lack of pity in the final act of vengeance, the murder of his brother's children: after the ritual of their murder, described in piteous detail by the Chorus, their limbs are served up as a feast to their father. In the English translation by Jasper Heywood (1561) an additional soliloquy was composed in which Thyestes appeals to the gods to avenge this atrocity.[4] Thus revenge continues in perpetuity.

In considering the horrific excesses of Senecan drama, it should be remembered that in the Renaissance Seneca was also admired for his loftiness of style, sententiousness and moral seriousness. Elizabeth I had translated from Seneca's plays and the English translation by Jasper Heywood of *Troas* was dedicated to her. Thomas Newton, in his admiring preface to *Tenne Tragedies*, warned against a literal reading of the plays without due attention to style and dramatic context:

> And whereas it is by some squeamish Areopagites surmised, that the reading of the tragedies, being interlarded with many phrases and sentences literally tending (at the first sight) sometime to the praise of ambition, sometime to the maintenance of cruelty, now and then to the approbation of incontinency, and here and there to the ratification of tyranny, can not be digested without great danger of infection: to omit all other reasons, if it might please them with no forestalled judgement to mark and consider the circumstances, why, where, and by what manner of persons such sentences are pronounced . . . For it may not be thought and deemed the direct meaning of Seneca himself, whose whole writings (penned with a peerless sublimity and loftiness of style) are so far from countenancing vice that I doubt whether there be any amongst all the catalogue of heathen writers that with more gravity of philosophical sentences, more weightiness of sappy words, or greater authority of sound matter beateth down sin, loose life, dissolute dealing, and unbridled sensuality: or that more sensibly, pithily, and bitingly layeth down the guerdon of filthy lust, cloaked dissimulation and odious treachery: which is the drift whereunto he leaveth the whole issue of each one of his tragedies.

Seneca's preoccupation with power and its corruption was only one aspect of his appeal to English Renaissance playwrights. His style was much admired and emulated; Kyd, Shakespeare and Marston draw on Seneca, either through direct citation, or through the use of set descriptive passages, the grieving lament and stichomythia. Formally, popular playwrights revealed an indebtedness to Seneca in their depictions of tormented or vindictive ghosts from the underworld, or through an appeal to mythic structures of relentless revenge.[5] We can see how the appeal to Seneca and the adaptation of Senecan material was a means of validating vernacular drama. Recourse to Seneca gave the new, popular and commercial Elizabethan theatre cultural capital.

Seneca's plays were read or performed under private auspices; that is, at court, at the inns of court and at the universities. *Oedipus* and *Medea* were read – or declaimed – in Latin and were possibly even treated to some kind of restricted performance in Cambridge colleges in the decades before Newton's edition.[6] Plays were also written at least partially in imitation of Seneca. Amongst the various entertainments, intellectual disquisitions and debates scheduled for Elizabeth I's visit to Oxford in 1564, there was a performance in the hall of Christ Church of a Latin play *Progne*, now lost.[7] The play was evidently a representation of the violent story told in the sixth book of Ovid's *Metamorphoses*, later to be evoked by Shakespeare in *Titus Andronicus*, in which Procne wrought revenge on her husband Tereus for his rape of her sister, Philomel. One of the students, Bereblock, described the play and his response to it:

> It is wonderful how she [Procne] longed to seek vengeance for the blood of her sister. She goes about therefore to avenge wrongs with wrongs, and injuries with injuries; nor is it all reverent to add crimes to crimes already committed . . . And the play was a notable portrayal of mankind in its evil deeds, and was for the spectators, as it were, a clear moral of all those who indulge too much either in love or in wrath, each of which even if they come to fairly good men nevertheless inflame them with too strong desire, and make them far fiercer and more ungovernable, and very different in voice, countenance, spirit, in word and deed, from moderation and self-control.[8]

What is interesting about this response is the moralistic tone, very much in keeping with the condemnations of anger and retaliation expressed in the essays of Seneca, Bacon and

Montaigne. Extreme emotions lead only to self-destruction. When revenge is transposed to the public theatres, however, it becomes more histrionic in its representation and, as dramatists recognized the potential in subverting the clear moralistic tone of earlier academic drama, the plight of the revenger came to elicit a more complex response.

Revenge was also a theme of Senecan academic plays, such as *Gorboduc*, performed before Queen Elizabeth in 1570 by the Gentlemen of the Inner Temple, and *The Misfortunes of Arthur* (1588), also performed at court. In the former play, drawing on the myth of Britain rather than classical mythology, the authors Thomas Sackville and Thomas Norton depict Gorboduc dividing his kingdom between his two sons, Ferrex and Porrex. Counsellors advise against such a policy, 'for with one land, one single rule is best' and, predictably, political anarchy follows. Ferrex, angry that his father, in dividing the kingdom, has ignored his alleged rights as elder son, vows to avenge the offence, but he is fatally pre-empted in his action: a messenger – following classical precedent in reporting violent acts – recounts the murder of Ferrex by Porrex, who now enters into sole possession of the realm. Gorboduc, in an appeal which will be reiterated time and again on the Elizabethan stage, calls on heaven for retributive justice and, amplifying his distress, invokes his own destruction: 'O Heavens, send down the flames of your revenge/ Destroy, I say, with flash of wreackful fire/ The traitor son, and then the wretched sire' (III. ii. 946–8). But such appeals are rhetorical only, as revenge is effected not by divine but by human agency. Videna, mother of Ferrex and Porrex, laments the death of Ferrex and, without any of the deliberation which will characterize later revenge plays, vows revenge on her son Porrex: 'To thine own flesh, and traitor to thyself,/ The gods on thee in Hell shall wreak their wrath/ And here in earth this hand shall take revenge' (IV. i. 1004–6). Porrex cannot hope to escape 'just revenge' and his murder at the hands of his mother is reported by Marcella, attendant to Videna. Cruelty of brother towards brother is now transmuted to that of mother against child in Marcella's lament: 'Will ever wight believe that such hard heart/ Could rest within the cruel mother's breast/ With her own hand to slay her only son' (IV. ii. 1234–6). *Gorboduc* represents what Bacon would have judged

21

public revenge in the sense that there is no secret plotting or devising of elaborate strategies; one action inexorably follows another. The play also presents the apparent complicity of divine and human agencies as Marcella bemoans the 'hard cruel heart' that could 'lend the hateful destiny that hand'. *Gorboduc*, admired by a neo-classicist such as Sir Philip Sidney for its tragic decorum and adherence to classical form, is a mythic antecedent for Shakespeare's more indeterminate *King Lear*. Any political message in Shakespeare's play remains open and opaque; not so in *Gorboduc*, which carries the clear political moral that lack of strength and unity at the centre of power will lead only to chaos in the realm, while the revenge theme carries an equally exemplary moral in its articulation of vengeance as unnatural, destructive and self-perpetuating.

THE SPANISH TRAGEDY

Twenty-nine performances of *The Spanish Tragedy* are recorded between 1592 and 1597: an impressive number exceeded only by two other plays – Christopher Marlowe's *Jew of Malta* and a lost play, *The Wise Man of West Chester* – according to extant records.[9] The continuing appeal of *The Spanish Tragedy* is recorded in the Induction to Ben Jonson's *Bartholomew Fair* (1614), where the scrivener reads a mock agreement, drawn up between the playwright and the audience: a pretext for Jonson to project an image of his ideal audience and of a critically discerning reception of his play. Consistency and constancy of judgement are to be commended: 'He that will swear *Jeronimo* or *Andronicus* are the best plays yet, shall pass unexpected at, here, as a man whose judgement shows it is constant, and hath stood still, these five and twenty, or thirty years'. *The Spanish Tragedy*, known here by the name of its protagonist Jeronimo or Hieronimo, is coupled with another, near contemporaneous, revenge tragedy, *Titus Andronicus*. Both are offered as examples of plays which have, despite competing dramatic aesthetics, retained their popularity and, in rather patronizing vein, the scrivener concludes that, while such taste in drama betokens a certain ignorance, 'it is a virtuous and staid ignorance'. If theatrical anecdotes can be credited, the popularity of *The*

Spanish Tragedy extended well beyond the composition of *Bartholomew Fair* and into the Caroline period. Richard Braithwait, in his book on female conduct, *The English Gentlewoman*, refers disapprovingly to women who make 'pleasure their vocation' and cites as example an occasion when a dying woman cried out vehemently for 'Hieronimo'.[10] That one of the earliest plays of the Elizabethan stage is recalled in a work which belongs to an era characterized by more elitist theatre, attests to the sustained theatrical impact of the play. The remarkable influence of *The Spanish Tragedy* is further borne out by its evocation in early revenge plays, as they notably trade on its success by displaying a similar concern with visual effects, detailed plotting, the portrayal of overwhelming emotion and an intense sense of injustice on the part of the protagonist.

Amongst other venues, the play was performed at the Rose playhouse owned by Philip Henslowe, the first of the theatres erected on the Bankside, which also doubled as a venue for bear and bull baiting. It is from Henslowe's records of performances and payments, his so called 'Diary', that we learn of the considerable number of revivals of the play.[11] The Rose playhouse was built in 1587 and, although we cannot say that the play was written with this venue specifically in mind, Kyd seems to have well understood the representational demands of the new theatrical space available to him; in particular, the art of constructing a play to be presented on the large, exposed stage of the amphitheatre (the Rose stage was wide, but shallow). *The Spanish Tragedy* is expressively theatrical in its dramatic exploitation of sensational spectacle and of the rhetorically patterned speech of lamentation and distraction. Departing from classical precedents, Kyd relies hardly at all on the indirect narration of his story by a Chorus or by messengers. The Chorus of *The Spanish Tragedy*, unseen spectators of action which has been predetermined, performs quite a different function. In the play proper, Kyd combines a complex plot of intrigue and, through Hieronimo's soliloquies, some sense of interiority which gives his drama a new psychological dimension and credibility.

As with subsequent revenge plays, and in contrast to the single narrative of most classical revenge tragedies, *The Spanish Tragedy* represents revenge and counter-revenge plots. The play

23

opens with the ghost of the Spanish knight Don Andrea, who informs us of his death in battle with the Portuguese, of his love for Bel-imperia, niece to the King of Spain, and, finally, his quest for revenge in the underworld. Andrea's desire for vengeance frames the play, but the dramatic focus shifts away from it to the alliance of Lorenzo, brother to Bel-imperia, and Balthazar, son of the Viceroy of Portugal, and their malicious machinations in murdering Horatio, friend to Andrea and son of Hieronimo. Knight Marshal of Spain. Balthazar and Lorenzo construe their murder of Horatio as revenge for Horatio's wooing of Bel-imperia. It is Bel-imperia, who for ambivalent motives initiates the love affair; but Lorenzo and Balthazar insist on seeing Horatio as challenging the play's rigid social hierarchy in his declarations of love, and they cruelly pun on his seeming aspiration as they hang up his body: 'Although his life were still ambitious, proud,/ Yet is he at the highest now he is dead' (II. iv. 59–60). Balthazar's readiness to act as an accomplice to the more sinister Lorenzo is explained by resentment and frustration which he glosses as revenge. Horatio's death prompts Hieronimo's vengeance, which, far from the dispassionate contrivance of Lorenzo and Balthazar, produces outraged suffering and moments of insanity. Further complications ensue with Lorenzo's intrigue to ensure that none of his accomplices in the murder of Horatio survive to betray him, and thus he engineers the deaths of Serberine and Pedringano. Lorenzo's double-dealing is in a sense replicated by Hieronimo's elaborate plotting of revenge during the performance of *Soliman and Perseda*, but in Hieronimo's case the double-dealing is more complex: those who profess themselves innocent – the actual murderers – play the murdered, unwittingly and in earnest.

The play encompasses pagan and Christian rhetoric for and against revenge. In a similar cultural cross-current, it juxtaposes, in the figures of the Chorus, the spirit of Revenge and the ghost of Andrea, intimates in the pagan underworld, with characters inhabiting Catholic Renaissance courts of Spain and Portugal. There might seem to be some conflict between the two dramatic constructs. In his soliloquy in Act 3, Hieronimo, presented as an apparent agent of free will, agonizes over whether to revenge or leave vengeance to God. Yet, from the opening chorus when Andrea tells us that Proserpine has granted him Revenge as his companion, we know that Revenge is scripting the tragedy. Revenge is directed and controlled by the powers of the underworld much as the Furies in classical plays determine retribution, and this mythic necessity is commensurate with Hieronimo's inner compulsion to revenge. Although in the Choruses at the end of each act Andrea expresses impatience at the leisurely way Revenge seems to be going about his purpose, Revenge's words to Andrea leave us in no doubt of the outcome. At the close of Act 2, Andrea is incredulous: not only has his own killing in battle not been acquitted, but his friend Horatio has now been murdered by Lorenzo and Balthazar. In a memorable image, Revenge intimates that events will take their prescribed course:

ANDREA. Broughtst thou me hither to increase my pain?
I looked that Balthazar should have been slain,
But 'tis my friend Horatio that is slain . . .
REVENGE. Thou talkest of harvest when the corn is green.

(II. v.1–6)

At the end of the third act, when Andrea is yet again importuning Revenge to awaken, Revenge reminds him that the characters are unconsciously fulfilling the destiny he has dictated: 'Behold, Andrea, for an instance how/ Revenge hath slept, and then imagine thou/ What 'tis to be subject to destiny.' Events in the Spanish court are not then simply historicized through the projection of the Spanish/Portuguese conflict; we are also encouraged to share the Chorus's perspective of an endless cycle of crime and retribution.

Being of the action but not in it, the Chorus occupies an ambiguous space that is open to definition in the performance of *The Spanish Tragedy*. Possibly in a gallery on high or standing at the side of the stage, even occasionally intermingling with the characters, Revenge is a constant reminder of an infernal presence and of the illusory nature of Hieronimo's apparent free will. Modern productions have made effective use of these two extra-dramatic characters, interweaving them into the stage action, visible – as is their purpose – only to the audience. There is an element not only of tension but of comedy between the impatient, incredulous Andrea and the laconic, deliberate Revenge who sleeps out part of the play's action. In the production staged in the small Cottesloe auditorium of the Royal National Theatre in 1982,[12] Revenge was there to prompt Hieronimo (Fig. 1). Clad in black leathers, suggesting both an executioner and an exhausted stage hand, and smoking cheroots, Revenge handed out the props of Bel-Imperia's letter and Hieronimo's dagger, while Don Andrea stood aghast at the tardiness of his work. Kyd presents what we might now see as a Brechtian effect in that the audience is distanced from the action; the play is a pageant working towards a foreseeable conclusion. The extremities of Hieronimo's passion also contribute towards this effect as his rhetorical expression makes us aware of the actor playing the part and thus our response shifts from empathy to understanding.

In Renaissance drama, relationships between literary texts are endemic as dramatists drew eclectically from a wide range of materials. In *The Spanish Tragedy* Kyd is clearly indebted to the plays of Seneca, not only – as in *Thyestes, Trojan Women, Agamemnon* and *Hercules Furens* – for his revenge theme, but also for the play's rhetorical style. Hieronimo's laments for the death of Horatio recall the sorrowing Hecuba's laments in *Trojan Women* for the downfall of Troy and the murder of her husband Priam. The passages descriptive of the underworld in the Chorus speeches of Don Andrea in *The Spanish Tragedy* are reminiscent of Theseus's account to Amphitryon of the inexorable torments of the underworld in *Hercules Furens*. In contrast to the more amplified speeches of lament and evocative description, Seneca also employs stichomythia, a quick-fire dialogue of repartee and rejoinder. Kyd lacks the occasion for this, but he would seem to like the effect, since he does something similar in the wooing of Horatio by Bel-imperia, during which the eavesdropping Balthazar and Lorenzo interject their own twisted interpretations. The latter, of course, go unheard and receive no reply, making their rejoinders asides; nevertheless the dialogue and interjections have the antagonist force typical of stichomythia.

In producing the first revenge tragedy of the popular theatre Kyd's debts were not only literary ones. *The Spanish Tragedy* has evident links with other cultural practices.[13] Both the place of execution and the platform where plays were performed were, in the early modern period, known as a scaffold. In *The Spanish*

Figure 1. Peter Needham as Revenge and Michael Bryant as Hieronimo in the 1982 Royal National Theatre production of Kyd's *The Spanish Tragedy*, directed by Michael Bogdanov. With the permission of the photographer Laurence Burns.

Tragedy the link between stage and scaffold is particularly apparent as Kyd constructs dramatic entertainment for the public theatre from the images of public execution. We could say that *The Spanish Tragedy* imaginatively represents part of public life where atrocity was acceptable. Hieronimo discovers the body of his son Horatio hanging in the bower where, like a common criminal, he has been strung up following the murder plot contrived by Lorenzo and Balthazar. That this image was central to the play's theatrical iconography is suggested by the woodcut on the title page of an edition of the play published in 1615 depicting the hanging corpse of Horatio in the bower (see frontispiece). The woodcut represents the figures of Hieronimo, bearing a sword and torch (to convey night on the undarkened stage), with the caption 'Alas it is my son Horatio'; Bel-imperia appealing to Hieronimo in the caption 'Murder, help Hieronimo'; and a masked Lorenzo holding Bel-imperia, with the words 'Stop her mouth'. The dramatic configuration relates to Act 2, scene 4, and compresses stage action: Hieronimo is not, of course, present at the murder of his son, nor are Bel-imperia and Lorenzo present at Hieronimo's discovery. Following the murder of Horatio, Bel-imperia is forcibly removed from the scene, leaving the stage ready for the shocking revelation to the father of the dead son. The image, on the other hand, brings together all the actors in the plots of murder and of retribution.

The scene of execution is re-enacted – this time in a scene of officially sanctioned justice – when Pedringano is executed for his murder of Serberine (following instructions from Lorenzo). The scene incorporates black humour as Pedringano on the scaffold persists in his belief that Lorenzo will intervene for his reprieve, jesting with the hangman and prompting his comment, 'Thou art even the merriest piece of man's flesh that e'er groaned at my office door' (III. vi. 80–81). In practice, gallows humour was not uncommon; prisoners would jest with the hangman or pun on their fate. But the most astonishing deployment of the scaffold image comes in the catastrophe, as Hieronimo, after wreaking destruction on the House of Castile, reveals both that the tragedy that they have witnessed is no mere spectacle and the part he has played:

> No, princes, know I am Hieronimo,
> The hopeless father of a hapless son,

Whose tongue is tuned to tell his latest tale. . .
Behold the reason urging me to do this!

(IV. iv. 82–7).

Here, the stage direction reads 'Shows his dead son', conveying the effect of Hieronimo drawing back a curtain which he had fastened up at the beginning of the previous scene, to expose the body of Horatio. Corpses of victim and murderer are simultaneously displayed; the sight of the bodies of Horatio and Lorenzo represents restored symmetry that is reinforced in Hieronimo's rhetorically patterned words.

It is possible to argue that Kyd panders to an audience's voyeuristic curiosity in the repeated use of the hanging, mutilated corpse in a manner reminiscent of the public executions at which they might equally be spectators. In Hamlet, a later revenge play that owes much to – but drastically departs from –The Spanish Tragedy, the corpses, until the catastrophe, lie hidden, undisclosed. Hamlet's father insists that what he undergoes in purgatory is too hideous to speak of. Kyd, on the other hand, presents death as grisly spectacle. The final Chorus, in projecting the fates of Lorenzo, Balthazar, Pedringano and Serberine, holds out the prospect of eternal torment as revenge is perpetuated ad infinitum. Death may appear to end their misery, but, concludes Revenge, 'I'll there begin their endless tragedy.' His words evoke the public execution where the purpose was to inflict torture and torment that would be replicated after death in the Hell of the damned. If there is an element of voyeurism, however, it is integrated into the drama as spectacle is consistently reinforced by the play's verbal effects. Visual and verbal images effectively complement each other throughout the play. Hieronimo crazily imagines a journey to the underworld, 'to th'Elysian plains', where he will recover his murdered son Horatio and his distraught determination to 'rip the bowels of the earth' is accompanied by the equally hysterical gesture of hacking at the stage with his dagger. By juxtaposing visual and verbal in this way there is an imaginative exploration of the nature of the violence to which Hieronimo is exposed and which he inwardly experiences.

Like Hamlet, Hieronimo's suffering leads him to contemplate suicide. It is characteristic of Kyd's style that, unlike Hamlet, Hieronimo's dilemma is externalized as he delivers his soliloquy on suicide with emblematic stage props. He enters (III. xii) carrying a poniard and rope and considers that his death would gain him entry to the underworld, where access to its monarch, Pluto, might give him the justice he has been denied on earth. But he draws back – 'Who will revenge Horatio's murder then?' – and in a symbolic gesture flings away the dagger and halter. A similar emblematic use of stage properties to articulate the protagonist's state of mind is evident in the following scene (III. xiii) when Hieronimo enters with a book in his hand. From the ensuing soliloquy it is not clear what the book is – a play (or the plays) of Seneca or the Bible, as he refers to both – and, true to the congruence in the play of pagan and Christian, he conflates classical stoicism and Biblical teaching in deliberating on his course of action. Should he leave vengeance to heaven which will not 'suffer murder unrepaid', and besides, 'Mortal men may not appoint their time'? Or, alluding to Seneca's play *Agamemnon*, should he 'strike, and strike home where wrong is offered thee'? In contrast with Hamlet's soliloquies, where so much remains unresolved and where any sense of resolution is negated by subsequent meditation, Hieronimo does resolve his dilemma and decides on a course of action:

> And, to conclude, I will revenge his death!
> But how? Not as the vulgar wits of men,
> With open, but inevitable ills,
> As by a secret, yet a certain mean,
> Which under kindship will be cloaked best.
>
> (III. xiii. 20–24)

Thus, indecision is temporary and Hieronimo embarks on a cunning strategy of revenge that will involve lulling his enemies into a false sense of security. In the next soliloquy, revenge – now 'sweet revenge' – is projected unequivocally as the only possible course of action. He reveals little of his plan, however, and the audience are kept guessing as to his strategy, so that it could be, as Isabella 'believes', that he has none at all.

As a tragic subject Hieronimo is characterized first by grief, then by his sense of inordinate injustice and mental suffering which lead to moments of madness. At the beginning of the play Hieronimo is clearly esteemed by the king, who is anxious that he be awarded the ransom money due to Horatio for his capture of Balthazar. Yet the king later accepts without question the words of his nephew Lorenzo, who dismisses Hieronimo as 'in a manner lunatic'; in the inflexible class structure of the play the word of royalty is taken before that of a loyal servant. In the early stages of the play his identity is indeed that of a dedicated servant to the crown. He sits in judgement on Pedringano for his murder of Serberine; he is faithful to the idea of full retribution and condemns Pedringano to death as a common criminal, to be hung on the scaffold. This brings a further reflection of Horatio's ignominious death and when Hieronimo observes 'This makes me to remember thee my son', his words carry more weight than he knows. The hanging corpse painfully reminds him of Horatio's similar fate, yet he is ignorant of the part Pedringano has played in Horatio's murder. His role as Knight Marshall is indeed ironic: he is an arbiter of justice, but for him justice is denied. He appeals to the highest authority, the king, for retribution for Horatio's murder; but his passionate out-pourings of loss and his manic gestures make it easy for Lorenzo to convince the king and court that, in coveting the ransom promised to Horatio, Hieronimo has become mad. His distracted pleas go unheeded amidst the formal court business and when justice through royal channels is denied him, Hieronimo sees private revenge as the only alternative. If he cannot find legal redress, he must become the executioner himself.

It could be argued that when Hieronimo embarks on revenge, which encompasses the innocent as well as the guilty, this marks a transition from heroic status to that of villain, but this seems rather too simplistic. Hieronimo's actions are grounded in moral deliberation; his compulsive responses are entirely credible, emanating first from grief and then from a sense of injustice. His soliloquy when he discovers his murdered son captures his distracted passions. As the elaborate conceits convey – eyes are 'fountains fraught with tears' – he is overwhelmed by sorrow. In the final scene, when the audience views Horatio's corpse, Hieronimo's speech carries the weight of emotion, expressive of unbearable loss and an aching need for retribution:

> See here my show, look on this spectacle!
> Here lay my hope, and here my hope hath end;
> Here lay my heart, and here my heart was slain;
> Here lay my treasure, here my treasure lost;

31

Here lay my bliss, and here my bliss bereft;
But hope, heart, treasure, joy, and bliss,
All fled, failed, died, yea, all decayed with this.
From forth these wounds came breath that gave me life;
They murdered me that made these fatal marks.
The cause was love, whence grew this mortal hate.

(IV. iv. 88–97)

Despite the verbal artifice in the use of alliteration and repetition, the emotion breaks through the formal patterning: the lines effectively convey the depths of suffering and encapsulate the extremities of love and hate which compel revenge. Hieronimo's heightened feelings are communicated in the distortion of his logical patterns of thought. Horatio's death is metaphorically the death of his father. The self-observation 'They murdered me that made these fatal marks' should rationally precede the impulse to revenge which has energized Hieronimo: 'From forth these wounds came breath that gave me life.' The point is simply made: love for Horatio breeds hatred for his killers.

Horatio's body is a constant reminder to his father of inner trauma, as well as a powerful symbol of murder and injustice. In *The Spanish Tragedy* physical objects are powerful mementoes and, like places, trigger memory of what has been lost. The napkin given to Horatio by Bel-imperia, who had received it from Andrea, serves this function. Hieronimo claims the napkin and with it mops up his son's blood on discovering the body in his bower. Subsequently, Isabella, before killing herself, razes the bower to the ground in an attempt to destroy the memory of – and avenge herself upon – the place where her son was murdered (IV. ii). The handkerchief, symbolic of love and death, is obsessively retained and produced at key moments in the drama. One particular episode illustrates the way Kyd uses his stage properties so effectively. In the midst of his soliloquy when he is meditating on the rights and wrongs of revenge, Hieronimo breaks off, hearing a noise. He is approached by three citizens and an old man. The citizens ask Hieronimo, in his position as Knight Marshal, to intervene on their behalf before the king. Hieronimo questions each of them and asks of the Old Man what is the cause of his supplication (Fig. 2). In what appears as a bizarre coincidence, one which is typical of

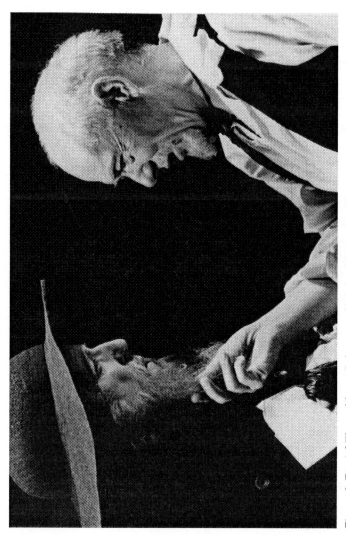

Figure 2. Daniel Thorndike as Balzuto and Michael Bryant as Hieronimo in the 1982 Royal National Theatre production of Kyd's *The Spanish Tragedy*, directed by Michael Bogdanov. With the permission of the photographer Laurence Burns.

the reflexive plots of several revenge plays, Hieronimo discovers that the Old Man too has a murdered son: 'What's here? The humble supplication/ Of Don Bazulto for his murdered son' (III. xiii. 78–9). Hearing of the Old Man's loss provokes in Hieronimo an extreme verbal and physical response: in his distracted state he conflates the two murdered sons, pronouncing in a torrent of grief, 'No sir, it was my murdered son,/ O my son, my son, O my son Horatio!' Regaining some composure, he comments in an oxymoron which conveys much about what Horatio's death has done to him that in Bazulto he sees a 'lively portrait of my dying self'. He offers Bazulto his 'handkerchief', actually the bloody napkin, recognizing it as the token of his commitment to revenge Horatio. In the final moments of the play the handkerchief is again displayed as a relic of remembrance in Hieronimo's stylized gesture, serving almost as an aide-memoir, as he tells his story to the survivors in the Spanish court:

> And here behold this bloody handkercher,
> Which at Horatio's death I weeping dipped
> Within the river of his bleeding wounds:
> It as propitious, see, I have reserved,
> And never hath it left my bloody heart,
> Soliciting remembrance of my vow
> With these, O these accursed murderers,
> Which, now performed, my heart is satisfied.

> (IV. iv. 121–28)

Emblematically, as well as verbally, the reference to the handkerchief would seem to convey Bacon's axiom that 'a man that studieth revenge keeps his own wounds green'. The napkin that Hieronimo has retained solicits vengeance. Yet the phrasing – 'And never hath it left my bloody heart' – also indicates that no external memento is needed: Hieronimo's heart is never anything but 'bloody' since Horatio's death. The handkerchief becomes a projection, a visible sign of grief and, as a stage prop, something to be held out and to be shown to an uncomprehending stage audience.

Revenge in *The Spanish Tragedy* is initially identified with justice; since, according to Hieronimo, justice has fled the earth, he must achieve it. But, as the final words of the above quotation convey, once justice is denied him, revenge, and his own death which must follow, are the only means whereby Hieronimo can allay his torment. Once his son's killers have been brought to justice through the ritual enactment of murder, Hieronimo's wounds, contrary to Bacon's diagnosis, can heal. Having enacted revenge, his last words before he bites out his tongue and kills himself reflect both his sense of requital and personal deliverance: 'Pleased with their deaths, and eased with their revenge/ First take my tongue, and afterwards my heart' (IV. iv. 190–91). Inner suffering can only be healed and closure effected through the wounds he inflicts and self-inflicts.

That the much-desired conclusion is effected through Hieronimo's play of *Soliman and Perseda* adds a further theatrical dimension to *The Spanish Tragedy* and provides a final instance of its exploitation of spectacle. The play creates a Russian doll-like effect as the audience witness the Chorus watching the Spanish court watching what they think is a play, but is in fact a ritual display of revenge. The on-stage audience of the Duke of Castile and the Viceroy applaud the supposed fictional murder of the characters their children are impersonating. Hieronimo stipulates that *Soliman and Perseda* should be performed in 'sundry languages' – a babbled performance. Since language at court is deceptive, babble, which means nothing and so cannot deceive, is more honest. To become a revenger one has to assume a role and in Hieronimo's case this is the only role with which at a given point he can easily identify. His son's murder has caused a loss of self and, again, revenge is the only way he can reclaim that lost self. In the violent, supposed linguistic chaos of court theatricals, in which Hieronimo plays his murderous part, he effects what he considers moral closure. In biting out his tongue, a last emblematic gesture, Hieronimo signifies that his sense of completion comes with the telling of his tale, and that done, neither he nor the audience has any further need of speech.

TITUS ANDRONICUS

Titus Andronicus, Shakespeare's first revenge play, has evident structural parallels with *The Spanish Tragedy*. Titus, like Hieronimo, is a public officer; both protagonists are loyal, in Titus's case ultra-loyal, servants of the state who, when unable to obtain justice, are driven to pursue private revenge. From being respected members of their communities (radically different as imperial militaristic Rome is from Renaissance Spain) they become liminal subjects and descend into fitful states of madness. In both plays the initial revenge plot is driven by mixed emotions and desires and then countered by another, motivated by a burning sense of injustice and eliciting a very different audience response. Like the Portuguese Balthazar in the Spain of *The Spanish Tragedy* Tamora, Queen of the Goths, and her sons, sometime enemies of Rome, are rewarded and assimilated into imperial culture, and, from a position of power within, plot revenge against the tribe responsible for their military abjection. The parallel is structural only. Balthazar follows Lorenzo's lead, whereas Tamora, her sons Chiron and Demetrius, and her lover, Aaron, actively conspire to destroy the Andronici: 'I'll find a way to massacre them all' (I. i. 450), Tamora assures the emperor, whose resentment of Titus makes him receptive to Tamora's deceit.

Revenge comes easily to the lips of the opponents of the Andronici; the slowness with which Titus moves towards revenge in comparison with Tamora, her sons, and Aaron differentiates the two factions. Nevertheless, it is Titus's ritualistic sacrifice of Tamora's son Alarbus to ensure that 'the groaning shadows' of his sons are appeased which initiates the Goths' revenge. Titus presents the ritual as sacrifice, but it is in truth an act of revenge against the enemy responsible for his sons' deaths. Jonathan Bate, the Arden editor of the play, comments that 'Rome prided itself on not allowing human sacrifice: this is the first sign that the city is becoming barbaric in its practices.'[14] In an attempt to persuade Titus Andronicus against the ritual, Tamora puts forward a powerful argument: Titus's triumph is manifest already and it needs no further demonstration; her sons fought for their country, as did his (I. i. 107–23). At the beginning and end of her speech, she argues for compassion. She asks him to feel as a father what she feels as a mother, and towards the end she invokes divine mercy as a human potential. Human nature, in showing mercy, draws near to the nature of the gods without risking hubris: 'Sweet mercy is nobility's true badge'. This speech, which momentarily blurs any distinction between pagan and Christian, seems, from the pagan Tamora, anachronistic. But, as we have seen in *The Spanish*

Tragedy, the coexistence of pagan and Christian language, iconography and typography is characteristic of these early revenge plays, heavily influenced as they are by Seneca and Ovid. Moreover, the speech illustrates how argument and rhetoric are employed in the play. Within minutes of her appeal to Titus to show mercy, one of her sons is looking forward to the 'opportunity of sharp revenge' for his brother, who has been duly killed, dismembered and offered as a sacrifice. Once she is in the powerful position of Saturninus's wife, Tamora speaks effortlessly with a forked tongue. In the hearing of the Andronici she takes their part – 'at my suit, sweet, pardon what is past' (I. i. 436) – and then, in an aside, swears vengeance. The situation is designed to emphasize the enormity of her double-dealing. Titus does not believe in pardoning wrong, nor does Tamora. The difference is that Tamora uses the language of forgiveness as an instrument of persuasion and as a way of ingratiating herself, always with the motive of revenge. The language of mercy deployed in the interests of violence and violation attains its ultimate ironic perversion in Chiron's reply to Demetrius's remark that he wishes to have a thousand Roman women to serve his lust: 'A charitable wish, and full of love' (IV. ii. 43). Forgiveness, charity and mercy enter the dramatic world of *Titus Andronicus* as cynical perversion and the only time the characters speak of forgiveness – and this is true of both revengers, Titus and Tamora – is when they are appealing to others to show the forgiving side of their natures.

The long history of critical disdain of *Titus Andronicus* – partly shaped by reaction against Titus's cannibalistic revenge, which has its origins in Ovid's *Metamorphoses* and Seneca's *Thyestes* – has been successfully challenged by later twentieth-century productions[15] and by the film *Titus* (directed by Julie Taymor). These productions have projected the sorrow and unbearable anguish experienced by Titus and his show of restraint before he is transformed by violence. Focusing on the final scenes of the play tends to distort the role of Titus as revenger. It is only after the mutilation of Lavinia, the execution of his two innocent sons, and the realization that his own self-mutilation to save them was in vain, that Titus emerges, and even then slowly, from his great abyss of suffering as an agent of revenge. While Tamora, her sons and Aaron speak and plot their revenge single-mindedly, Titus resists the idea, resorting to ineffectual means of relief and redress. The nearest he comes initially to revenge is through displacement, when he condones his brother Marcus's killing of a fly after being told 'it was a black ill-favoured fly, like to the empress' Moor' (III. ii. 67–8).

As in *The Spanish Tragedy*, the first part of the play presents the confusion and suffering of the protagonist, ignorant of the identity of his enemy. Titus loses faith in Roman justice and this is conveyed in the remarkable moment when he turns from pleading before the Tribunes for his sons' lives to spontaneous outpouring of grief and despair:

> . . . If they did hear,
> They would not mark me, or if they did not mark,
> They would not pity me, yet plead I must,
> And bootless unto them.
> Therefore I tell my sorrows to the stones,
> Who, though they cannot answer my distress,
> Yet in some sort they are better than the tribunes
> For that they will not intercept my tale.

(III. i. 33–40)

In his unheard appeal, his sorrow at the lack of human pity, and, then, his desperate appeal to the stones, there is much pathos. Yet, as with the Senecan avenger, there is no redirecting of experience; Titus's grief does nothing to soften his vengeful thoughts, which surface as, if anything, more cruel and malevolent.

Once Lavinia, through turning the pages of Ovid's *Metamorphoses* to the rape of Philomel, reveals what has happened to her and then writes the names of the rapists in the sand, Titus is in a position to right his family's wrongs. In a ritualistic act, Marcus bids Titus and his children kneel and vow 'That we will prosecute by good advice/Mortal revenge upon these traitorous Goths/ And see their blood, or die with this reproach' (IV. i. 92–4). Yet, Titus remains too distracted by grief to act. Echoing Hieronimo, he declares that justice has fled the earth and must be found elsewhere. He instructs his family to search for justice in the underworld. In a heavily symbolic scene, his nephew, apparently responding to the command, urges Titus to act: 'Pluto sends you word/ If you will have Revenge from hell, you shall.' In a deranged gesture reminiscent of Hieronimo's

38

hacking at the bowels of the earth in his quest for justice, Titus shoots arrows to the gods soliciting justice 'to wreak our wrongs'. Yet, while sending his surviving son to court with thinly veiled messages for Chiron and Demetrius that their crimes are known, Titus still resists active retaliation. Marcus appeals for cosmic justice, betraying some frustration at Titus's restraint:

> O heavens, can you hear a good man groan
> And not relent or not compassion him?
> Marcus, attend him in his ecstasy
> That hath more scars of sorrow in his heart
> Than foeman's marks upon his battered shield,
> But yet so just that he will not revenge.
> Revenge the heavens for old Andronicus!
>
> (IV. i. 123–9)

The weight of Titus's suffering, 'his scars of sorrow', disables any reaction. Titus's response to some extent fits Freud's description of mourning in his thesis 'Mourning and Melancholia', in that the crushing burden of bereavement traps him in a forest of desolation, unable to act, and unable to express his loss other than in an abstracted manner.[16]

When he does begin to formulate his revenge against the Goths, Titus's deranged words and actions convince Tamora that the aged warrior is an enervated opponent. The two revenge plots coalesce in Tamora's bizarre attempts to ensnare Titus, suggesting that the pursuit of revenge has also affected her judgement. Dressed as Revenge personified, Tamora confronts Titus as a potential accomplice: 'Tell him Revenge is come to join with him/ And work confusion on his enemies' (V. ii. 7–8). Titus sees through the preposterous disguise and only then is he galvanized into outmanoeuvring the Goth and devising his grotesque retaliation: 'I knew them all, though they supposed me mad,/And will o'erreach them in their devices' (V. ii. 142–3). Overreaching in retaliation, surpassing the original crime, is a feature of Senecan revenge. Before he cuts the throats of Chiron and Demetrius, Titus declaims his intent to exceed in cruelty the revenge of Progne on her husband Tereus for the rape and mutilation of her sister: 'For worse than Philomel you used my daughter,/ And worse than Progne I will be revenged' (V. ii. 194–5). Titus's response exemplifies the fundamental condition of the revenger: the more one is violated, the more violent the reprisal. The enactment of his final revenge in the preparation and serving of the cannibalistic feast outdoes Atreus's similar act reported in *Thyestes*, as well as that of Progne's revenge against Tereus. It reveals the metamorphosis of Titus into a state of monstrous cruelty:[17] a change which may have influenced similar transportations of violence in the persons of Vindici in *The Revenger's Tragedy* and Antonio in *Antonio's Revenge*. The change in Titus is much less consciously histrionic than that of Antonio and it does not invite moral judgement. In *Titus Andronicus* the act of revenge exposes no deliberation and no moral dimension. The centre of the drama is elsewhere as Shakespeare makes the transformation of the protagonist entirely credible. The interest in Titus as he is altered from unswerving defender of Rome to the nemesis of its extended imperial family is psychic, not moral.

HAMLET

Around a decade separates Shakespeare's two revenge plays *Titus Andronicus* and *Hamlet*, and in almost every aspect of their style, tone and theatrical effect the plays could not be more different. The resemblance of *Hamlet* to earlier revenge plays is indeed superficial; it does, however, follow the pattern of its predecessors in structuring the drama on multiple plots of revenge. Old Hamlet's killing of Old Fortinbras in single combat, which we hear about in the opening scene of the play, provokes the play's first strategy of revenge as Young Fortinbras plans his campaign against Denmark. This is soon pushed to the margins of the play, however, after the astonishing appearance of the Ghost of Old Hamlet to his son in the final scene of the first act (Fig. 3). The Ghost is majestic, sorrowful, tormented, quite unlike any Senecan or neo-Senecan fury, yet its message is unequivocal: Hamlet must keep faith with the dead and revenge his father's murder.[18]

As the extensive critical and creative afterlife of *Hamlet* attests, Shakespeare created an extremely complex revenger with a developed self-consciousness unlike any revenge play protagonist that came before or after.[19] Grieving for the death of his

Figure 3. David Burke as the Ghost in the 1989 Royal National Theatre production of *Hamlet*, directed by Richard Eyre. With the permission of the photographer John Haynes.

father and shocked by the hasty remarriage of his mother, Hamlet is further traumatized by the appearance of the Ghost. Hamlet's immediate response when the Ghost speaks of a murder 'most foul, strange and unnatural' is to ask the murderer's name, 'that ... I may sweep to my revenge' (I. v. 31). There is no hesitation as he speaks of himself as an avenging angel, sweeping 'with wings as swift/ As meditation or the thoughts of love'. His identification with his murdered father is immediate and complete. Yet, a little later, he recoils from the act: 'The time is out of joint. O cursed spite,/ That ever I was born to set it right' (I. v. 196–7). The shock of revelation prompts the first impulsive response; but, by the time he is able to say 'O cursed spite', Hamlet has recognized the full burden of revenge. His speculative cast of mind takes him beyond the act of revenge in killing Claudius: it has become a matter of setting right something that is out of joint in this place, at this time.

As avenger, Hamlet contrasts with Laertes, who, when Polonius is killed by Hamlet, finds himself, unknowingly, in the same position as his opponent. But Laertes embraces his role. When he learns that Hamlet has returned to Elsinore he sees his opportunity to requite the deed:

> But let him come.
> It warms the very sickness in my heart
> That I shall live and tell him to his teeth,
> 'Thus diest thou'.
>
> (IV. vii. 53–6).

Laertes employs the fierce, physical imagery of requital and is ready to become an avenger. But Claudius tests Laertes's rhetoric and the depth of his feelings for his father, asking him, 'What would you undertake/ To show yourself in deed your father's son/More than in words?' To which Laertes replies that he would cut Hamlet's throat in the church (IV. vii. 123–5). Seemingly, he enjoys the prospect of the revenger's part. Hamlet, though, as his reaction to the Ghost evinces, is divided within himself and the contradictions, which he never really resolves, prepare the audience for something other than a linear narrative of revenge.

The first act of *Hamlet* consists of dramatic exposition, although so intricately done that we are not aware of it as such.

The urgent injunction of the Ghost might seem to be providing momentum for future action, but it does not. Instead we have a digressive dramatic narrative in which the protagonist's need to revenge is subsumed by other concerns. In the discursive action of the middle acts, the sequence of events is less significant than what is happening simultaneously. The time-scale of the play from the appearance of the Ghost to the murders of Hamlet and, in hasty retribution, of Claudius can be estimated at a few months, but it could be said that the play creates a different sense of transition. As has been discussed by Barbara Everett, we feel a more extensive period of time elapsing as Hamlet ages from a young student, fresh from Wittenberg, to the mature, 30-year-old man of the graveyard scene. On his return to Elsinore from England, having escaped the death plotted for him by Claudius, aided by the unsuspecting Rosencrantz and Guildenstern, Hamlet seems to have matured.[20] He feels uneasy at the prospect of the duel with Laertes and yet there is a quiescence in his words, with their biblical resonance, spoken to Horatio: 'The readiness is all. Since no man, of aught he leaves, knows aught, what is't to leave betimes? Let be' (V. ii. 218–20). By returning to Elsinore in the knowledge that Claudius knows that Hamlet knows he is a murderer and has already plotted his death, Hamlet comes back facing the prospect of his own death. At this point it would seem that Hamlet has forgotten his obligation to revenge his father or that it is submerged in his providential cast of thought.

Rather than consider the central acts following the Ghost's injunction to revenge in temporal sequence, it is more helpful to think of them in spatial terms. The play occupies very distinct spaces – the court, personal space and private space – and these would have been effectively created on the open, bare and fluid space of the Elizabethan stage. From the start Hamlet distances himself from the busy life of the court and its world of dissembling; consequently, court scenes often take place without him. Hamlet's sense of disgust at Claudius's speciousness and his obsequious courtiers is unmistakable and, although the audience perceive corruption in the spying which is prevalent in Elsinore and in Claudius's manipulative rhetoric at the beginning of the play, the sense of turpitude is mostly Hamlet's. From everything he says we gather he has always had a poor opinion of his uncle: his response to the Ghost's revelations – 'O my prophetic soul! My uncle?' – shows that he has long included his uncle's perfidious nature in his sense of human possibility (although nothing has prepared him for his mother's behaviour).

Hamlet's personal space is occupied together with Horatio, perhaps the only person he trusts in Elsinore, and briefly with his mother when he confronts her in her closet. When with Ophelia, Hamlet is always in court and on his guard. The scene in which Polonius and Claudius spy on Hamlet – the so-called nunnery scene – might recall in form the scene in *The Spanish Tragedy* in which Lorenzo and Balthazar eavesdrop on Belimperia and Horatio. But the tone and tenor of the scene in *Hamlet* is quite different: as Hamlet almost certainly directs his quips, barbs, evasions and provocations at the eavesdroppers as much as at Ophelia. Private space is entirely Hamlet's and revealed through his soliloquies. Although Kyd allows some access to the tormented, obsessive psyche of the revenger, the interiority is much more developed in *Hamlet*. In four major soliloquies Shakespeare has created an intense inner drama as thought process becomes theatre and unresolved dramatic and metaphysical tensions are disclosed. Hamlet explores the recesses of self; feelings overlap and feed on one another and take over the mind. Such tendencies run counter to the single-minded purpose which must be that of the revenger and to what we see in the play's other revengers, Laertes, Fortinbras and the Pyrrhus brought to life in the player's speech as the slayer of Priam.

Much has been written about Hamlet's apparent delay in taking revenge. Apart from the Ghost's admonition when he appears – or at least Hamlet thinks he appears – in Gertrude's closet and refers to Hamlet's 'almost blunted purpose' (III. iv. 111), the evidence for Hamlet's delays is found in the soliloquies. In fact, there is comparatively little delay, given the enormity of the task (Vindici in *The Revenger's Tragedy* waits nine years, but finds no reason to reproach himself); Hamlet's self-chiding would seem to be an aspect of his ambivalent response to revenge adumbrated in his first encounter with the Ghost. The inner space of the soliloquies is inseparable from Hamlet's divided conscience. Moments of detachment are conveyed almost simultaneously with self-reproach leading to impulses towards revenge. On the way to England, in effect as Claudius's prisoner, Hamlet encounters the captain of Fortinbras's army, who tells him that they are fighting 'to gain a little patch of ground/ That hath in it no profit but the name./ To pay five ducats – five – I would not farm it.' (IV. iv. 18–20). At first Hamlet expresses the detached view that sees Fortinbras and others as ready to kill and be killed 'even for an eggshell'; but this is followed by yet another avowal to revenge: 'O from this time forth,/ My thoughts be bloody, or be nothing worth!' The double vision in the soliloquy is emphasized by the context in which it is spoken. Hamlet castigates himself for not revenging: 'I do not know/ Why yet I live to say 'This thing's to do',/ Sith I have cause, and will, and strength, and means to do't.' Yet at this point, as Claudius's prisoner, he is at his most impotent. It is more significant that only hours earlier he has killed Polonius believing that he was the king. His self-castigation appears to be unfounded, either utterly subjective or indicative of a sense of duty he cannot relate to.

Unlike other revenge tragedies, *Hamlet* contains very little elaborate, sustained intrigue or adoption of role-playing. Hieronimo, Titus and Vindici in *The Revenger's Tragedy* plot and scheme to ensnare and destroy their opponents. The nearest Hamlet gets to calculated plotting is his devising of a play which he hopes will 'catch the conscience of the king': that is, prove unequivocally that the Ghost is right and that Claudius is a murderer. The reaction of Claudius to the performance of 'The Murder of Gonzago' does prove his guilt (Fig. 4), but Hamlet's action here, as a more wily avenger would have recognized, is counterproductive, alerting Claudius to Hamlet's dangerous knowledge. Hamlet's 'antic disposition' reflects an aspect of the deception of the revenger, but again it is given more profound significance. One of the many questions this play raises relates to whether Hamlet's madness is always a pretence or whether hysteria lies behind the simulation. The mercurial character of Hamlet offers so many possibilities and actors have variously interpreted the degree and extent of Hamlet's condition, showing him shifting between real and feigned madness, apparently unaware of the transition between them.[21] The twilight zone in which Hamlet exists is a more

Figure 4. John Castle as Claudius and Sylvia Sims as Gertrude in the 1989 Royal National Theatre production of *Hamlet*, directed by Richard Eyre. With the permission of the photographer John Haynes.

subtle variation of Hieronimo's distracted grief which leads to alternate moments of insanity and lucidity of purpose and of Titus's generalized, unfocused mourning. Hamlet's antic disposition is ostensibly calculated to give him freedom of word and action, his disguise being a way of securing his impunity. But we do not know whether Hamlet is indeed deranged by his tragic burden or whether he is assuming this condition, and there is no way of knowing. It is even possible to imagine that he does not know himself; he could assume a role and then be overtaken by it, or he could be moving between pretence and actuality.

There is very little in Hamlet's role or self-definition that identifies him with other avengers. He recognizes, once he knows the murderer is the king, the need for secrecy and even dissimulation, but he has no need of intrigue or disguise other than the cloak of madness, in order to gain access to the king. In *The Revenger's Tragedy* we see Vindici plotting and deceiving in order to enter the Duke's inner circle and then lure him to his death. The brief reported episode of the deaths of Rosencrantz and Guildenstern, in which Hamlet opens a sealed document and forges another in its place, sending the pair to their execution in England, aligns Hamlet briefly with the intrigues of other revengers. Yet here such resemblance is superficial: Hamlet is convinced that they have conspired against his life, while the audience sees them more as the king's dupes than his agents.

As a revenge tragedy, *Hamlet* has a failed climax; namely, the moment when, following the players' scene which has proved the king's guilt to him, Hamlet comes across Claudius praying with his back to him (Fig. 5). Claudius knows nothing of Hamlet's presence and Hamlet nothing of Claudius's failed act of penitence: 'My words fly up, my thoughts remain below./ Words without thoughts never to heaven go' (III. iv. 97–8). Hamlet's ostensible reason for not killing Claudius reflects the mindset of a more conventional revenger bent on achieving full retribution. He relishes the thought of killing Claudius when he is deep in sin so that 'his heels may kick at heaven'. The text gives us no clue whether other compunctions may underlie Hamlet's resistance to killing a defenceless, praying man. Certainly, there is little remorse when, shortly after, he kills

Figure 5. John Castle as Claudius and Daniel Day-Lewis as Hamlet in the 1989 Royal National Theatre production of *Hamlet*, directed by Richard Eyre. With the permission of the photographer John Haynes.

the wrong man, Polonius, believing him to be the king. When Hamlet does kill Claudius, it is without forethought when, wounded by Leartes's envenomed sword, his imminent death makes filial duty inescapable. It is an act as much in retaliation for the accidental poisoning of his mother and he does not refer explicitly to his father in the final moments of the play as Hieronimo speaks of his son, Horatio. This has prompted some critics to question whether Hamlet is indeed thinking about his father when he completes the task.[22] But remembrance is surely embedded in Hamlet's words: 'Here, thou incestuous, murderous, damned Dane'; and requital when, in forcing poison down Claudius's throat, he comes close to enacting the original crime. To ensure that his act of regicide is known to be an act of vengeance and an instrument of justice, Hamlet has to ask Horatio to 'report me and my cause aright'. This 'aright' is the necessary complement to the 'right' in the penultimate line of Act 1 ('O cursed spite/ That ever I was born to set it right'). Only when Horatio has done this, and not before, will the business of revenge be satisfactorily completed and order restored. But with the death of Hamlet, who in Fortinbras's words was likely 'had he been put on,/ To have proved most royal', the price of revenge is seen as a terrible one. No other revenge play discards the standard mechanisms to such a degree, and none conveys such a powerful sense of loss.

THE TRAGEDY OF HOFFMAN OR A REVENGE FOR A FATHER

The Tragedy of Hoffman by Henry Chettle was published only in 1631, although it is usually thought to have been performed shortly after the first productions of *Hamlet*, c.1601.[23] According to details on the title page of the published text, the play had been acted and well received at the Phoenix, a small indoor theatre in Drury Lane patronized by the gentry. The Caroline revival of a tragedy designed for the very different Elizabethan open-air popular theatre is a clear illustration of the enduring appeal of revenge plays: few plays could be said to reduce revenge to its stark essentials as *Hoffman* does. Intricate plotting; the madness of the principal female character, Lucibella the imbecility of the Duke's son Jerom who has been a student at

Wittenberg, and the adoption of multiple disguises to further intrigue, all suggest that Chettle was recalling specific theatrical formulas from Shakespeare and Kyd. Nothing, however, illustrates the differences in kind between tragedies of revenge more than a comparison between *Hoffman* and the work of his contemporaries.

Clois Hoffman is convinced that his father has been wrongfully executed and is, almost from the onset, ferociously bent on revenge that, he insists, must outdo his father's punishment. Hoffman's father, formerly Vice-Admiral of the Duke of Luningberg, had turned pirate, but was captured and put to death by having his brains burned out with an iron crown. The singular ferocity of *Hoffman* is located in this excruciating punishment, which understandably provokes Hoffman's relentless fury. Yet the play offers very little psychological insight. Although there is an immediate allusion to *Hamlet* in Hoffman's opening soliloquy as he registers his deep melancholy and chides himself for being tardy in a cause which 'justice and a father's death excites', the soliloquy is less an interior monologue and more a statement of identity and resumé of events. Chettle strives instead for theatrical effect: Hoffman interprets the peals of thunder and the lightning which accompany his soliloquy as divine disapproval of his failure to act. His melancholy dissipates as he determines to revenge his father's death. Addressing the flayed corpse of his father which he has stolen from the gallows, Hoffman vows to repay and replicate this public, institutionalized retribution with private revenge: 'I will not leave thee, until like thy self,/ I've made thy enemies, then hand in hand/ We'll walk to paradise' (ll. 23–5). He accepts that his own death is the corollary to the gratification of vengeance, but more immediate is the psychology of excess in the idea that revenge so justifies multiple murder that it leads to paradise.

Hoffman displays no divided purpose and, while the plot is elaborately conceived, the play is driven by the protagonist's desire for ritual closure. In the first acts of *The Spanish Tragedy* the audience are allowed to comprehend the injustice of Hieronimo's situation and the enormity of his suffering. In *Hoffman*, however, the justice or injustice of the fate of Hoffman's father is not established, nor are there are any glimpses of the protagonist's identity before and beyond the revenge plot. Everything is focused on the ways and means of wreaking revenge. In his desire to destroy not only the Duke but all those associated by blood guilt with him, Hoffman articulates the harshest of revenge codes. In the first scene the son of the Duke, Prince Otho, and his servant Lorrique are conveniently shipwrecked near Hoffman's hide-out and this affords Hoffman his first opportunity for redress. Momentarily he articulates a sense of loss as he persuades Lorrique to become an accomplice – 'Wouldst thou having lost a father as I have/ Whose very name dissolves my eyes to tears' (ll. 64–5) – yet his grief and loss become totally submerged in the vicious execution of revenge. Otho, in his turn, is tortured with the scorching crown: 'My father felt this pain, when thou hadst pleasure' (l. 218). Hoffman, addressing his father's hanging skeleton, ritualistically offers up Otho's corpse to him. The notions of equity and retribution are strongly and visually communicated in the stage action as Hoffman suspends Otho's flayed body next to that of his father.

Following this sensational opening, with its evocation of stage as scaffold, the play is taken over by Hoffman's intrigues against Otho's uncle, Ferdinand, Duke of Prussia, and rulers in alliance with him. His next move is to infiltrate the court and plot against Ferdinand and his heir, Jerom, whom Ferdinand dismisses as a 'witless fool'. Like Hamlet, Jerom has assumed imbecility, although there is no comparable motive and no psychological depth, in that his feigned madness never borders on real derangement. Jerom is disinherited so that Otho – in fact Hoffman in disguise – can become Prussia's heir. From this position Hoffman plots the murder of Lodowick, son of the Duke of Saxony, in revenge against the Duke, simply because he was present at the overthrow of Hoffman's father and to that extent acquiesced in it. Murder is twisted without being complex, as Hoffman schemes to eliminate everyone associated with his father's death.

Anticipating the success of his murderous intrigue, Hoffman justifies his act to Lorrique:

> When I have summ'd up my account of death
> And robbed those fathers of their lives and joy,
> That robbed me of my joy, my father's life . . .

We'll walk and meditate
And boast in the revenges I have wrought.

(ll. 729–33)

Clearly, what drives the revenger here is not the notion of restoring balance, but a sense of outrage that sweeps aside the pedantry of equivalence. Although he never forgets the purpose of his actions, Hoffman exhibits a grotesque version of self-fulfilment as he identifies absolutely with the act of murder. Revenge becomes self-compensation as he declares 'Revenge hath made me great by shedding blood', while Lorrique recognizes that in being Hoffman's accomplice he has entered into an empowering and demonic pact: 'I am half a monarch: half a fiend.'

As Hoffman overreaches himself in his designs, finally plotting to seduce Martha, wife of Luningberg and mother to Otho, Chettle imports some of the elements of *de casibus* tragedy, a medieval tragic form which depicted the rise and fall of over-ambitious subjects. When Martha discovers the scourged body of her son, she is driven to revenge and is herself metamorphosed in the process, mirroring what Hoffman has gone through before the play begins. In the first act of the play Hoffman recalls that Martha pleaded in vain with her husband to allow Hoffman to remove and retain the bones of his father. But once she is exposed to the grisly spectacle of her son's skeleton hung by the side of Hoffman's father, she knows only revenge: 'Well, I that never knew revenge's power,/ Have entertained her newly in my breast/ Determine what's to do' (ll. 2167–9). A little later, when Saxony invites comment on the ingeniousness of their plot against Hoffman, she states that she will comply with 'any thing however desperate'. In another instance of Chettle's manipulation of stage image, Martha commands her accomplices to kneel, lay their hands on the head of Lorrique, who has betrayed Hoffman, and swear 'vengeance against Hoffman'.

As in earlier plays, revenge begets a counter-plot; Hoffman has worked many deaths by his deceit and intrigues, and Martha retaliates by emulating his trickery and, with her accomplices, ensnaring Hoffman to his death. Private and public revenge become homologous as Hoffman is tortured in the same manner as he had tortured Otho. 'Revenge should have proportion' (l. 2200), decrees Mathias, brother of the murdered Lodowick. Although when he says this he has something else in mind, proportionate revenge is perpetrated in an exact sense: the Duke of Saxony calls for the burning crown and in the final scene of the play Hoffman defiantly prepares to meet the same fate as his enemy. Whether Hoffman's quest is justified or not, the play never really answers. The only means he has are private and, if we equate him in this respect with his dead father, 'piratical', outside the law. Martha, on the other hand, as ruler, embodies the law, and her revenge materializes as state punishment. Anarchy and autocracy are seen thus to overlap.

As is clear from the opening stage direction, when Hoffman reveals the hanging cadaver of his father, *Hoffman* enlists the visual effects of a theatre of blood. His father's skeleton is a constant reminder to Hoffman to revenge and – in his grim metaphor of retribution – the bones will not be interred until he has made a deep enough 'incision' in the bodies of his enemies. As with the hanging corpse of Horatio in *The Spanish Tragedy*, the suspended anatomies of Hoffman's father and Otho suggest that the Elizabethan theatre was consciously re-presenting the theatre of punishment orchestrated by the state. Hieronimo, Hoffman and Martha are all incensed that their kin have been treated as no more than common criminals and this thought further fuels their revenge. As a rule the criminal's body was left in its chains as a warning to spectators of the consequences of crime and treason. On the stage, however, the constantly present, if concealed, cadavers do not serve the same admonitory purpose. They are instead emblematic of inner trauma, constantly reminding the revengers of their duty; thus, the refusal to inter bodies and bones until revenge has been effected.

If in its stage images *Hoffman* evokes the public execution, it is also theatrically self-reflexive, as the play, very knowingly, plays with play-acting. Revenge is driven by a prescribed plot and Hoffman never doubts his ascribed role. After he has strung up the corpse of Otho, he draws the curtain, declaring that he will shut the stage up now that 'one act is done'. Later he urges Lorrique to play his 'part' in poisoning the Duke of Prussia, describing the act as 'our tragedy's best heart', and appeals to revenge, his 'scarlet mistress', to applaud the ingeniousness of his plot. Placing himself in the mainstream of literary revengers, Hoffman remarks that his revenge will surpass that of Thyestes, Tereus, Jocasta and Medea. In alerting an audience to such bloody precedents, Chettle does not confound its expectations. As with other avengers, revenge for Hoffman is compulsive. Yet the play reduces revenge to its essentials, as we see Hoffman, his personality warped by his savage obsession, plotting the violent elimination of everyone associated with his father's death. There is no frustrated quest for justice and consequently the play elicits a less ambivalent response than *The Spanish Tragedy* or *Titus Andronicus*.

The *Tragedy of Hoffman* is shaped by the protagonist's fierce single-mindedness and consequently, of all revenge plays, it presents us with the rawest images of revenge and its ramifying havoc. When Hoffman's actions are revealed, Martha and her accomplices enter his world, emulate his pretences and demand to match his actions with deliberate, calculated reprisal. As rulers, instead of leading Hoffman into an ambush, they could presumably use the power of the state to bring Hoffman to justice. Chettle's plot, however, conforms to the symmetry of the revenge code. Thus, the play appears to conform with patterns of expectation that are theatrical, not psychological.

2

Revenge and Metatheatricality

Several years separate John Marston's *Antonio's Revenge* and a play of uncertain authorship, *The Revenger's Tragedy*, the two plays to be discussed in this chapter. The location of each is Italy and, as in subsequent revenge plays, the popular image of Italy promoted in prose and drama, as locus of political corruption, is exploited to produce a spectacular celebration of revenge. Such a heightened perception was informed by the reputations of such families as the Borgias, Sforzas and Medici who held power in the city states; but the view was shaped also by native hostility and the impulse to demonize Italy as the fount of Catholicism. While *Antonio's Revenge* and, to a lesser extent, *The Revenger's Tragedy* pioneer Italy as location of revenge drama, in keeping with the outrageous energies of the plays, Italy is much more a fantastic place of the mind than the more material settings in the plays of Webster, Ford and the later Middleton. More than a sense of place, however, what conjoins *Antonio's Revenge* and *The Revenger's Tragedy* is their self-conscious theatricality and their sense of play. The two works draw attention to their status as revenge drama through melodramatic exaggeration and parody of the elements of earlier tragedies and through verbal echoes of the language of revenge. Notably, both works exemplify the essentially non-naturalistic nature of revenge plays as transparent, self-confessed villains eagerly reveal their infamy to the audience. Spectators are placed in a uniquely privileged position: the stage is a world which they know intimately, yet from this safe distance they can applaud or relish or deplore successive acts of villainy.

ANTONIO'S REVENGE

Unlike his precursors in revenge drama, Marston was university educated. Having graduated from Oxford, he entered Middle Temple to study law, a pursuit which he abandoned in order to write first poetry and then drama.[1] He began his career as a verse satirist and the satiric impulse is retained in the plays he wrote for child actors in the first decade of the seventeenth century. Competition from children's companies – effectively choristers – seems to have been a source of professional anxiety for the adult players and the playwrights who wrote for them. In *Hamlet*, as the troop of players arrive in Elsinore to perform at court, Rosencrantz tells the Prince of the decline in the players' popularity through changes in theatrical taste: 'an eyrie of children, little eyases, that cry out on the top of question, and are most tyrannically clapped for't' (II. ii. 337–9). The comment is superfluous to the dramatic scene and represents a topical allusion to the activities of the recently revived companies of boy actors, the Children of Paul's and the Children of the Chapel, and the professional rivalry of dramatists writing for the adult companies and the children's companies. *Antonio's Revenge* reduces to parody certain aspects of revenge drama highly successful in the commercial theatre and thus it can be seen as ammunition in the competition between playing companies and their affiliated playwrights.

Paul's Boys were revived in 1599[2] and amongst the first plays to be performed were Marston's tragicomic *Antonio and Mellida* and its sequel *Antonio's Revenge*. We do not know for certain whether or not *Hamlet* was performed before *Antonio's Revenge*, although there is some evidence that it was.[3] Marston's histrionic treatment of revenge, at times approaching burlesque, is very different from Shakespeare's subtle psychological and philosophical exploration in *Hamlet*. Yet, a broad comparison of the two plays suggests that Marston appropriated from Shakespeare dramatic topoi to project an individual reworking of themes and motifs. Both plays represent the scenario of a son mourning the death of his father, who appears as a ghost enjoining the son to revenge, and in both plays the murderer desires the wife of the ruler he has killed. But only in the barest of outlines can these two revenge plays, produced so close in time to one another, be compared. The ghost of Hamlet's father who dominates the first act of the tragedy is a restless, tormented soul from purgatory who strikes fear in the hearts of the soldiers on watch. Although the Ghost elicits a promise from his reluctant son to remember him and avenge his death, he has to reappear later to remind Hamlet of his purpose. The ghost of Andrugio also appears to his son Antonio in the churchyard, calling on Antonio to revenge his blood. Antonio betrays none of Hamlet's trauma, and his subsequent exchange with his mother draws attention to the play's artifice as he declaims rhetorically in Latin, quoting from Seneca's *Thyestes*. In no time Antonio has formulated his gruesome revenge. As in *Hamlet*, the ghost of the murdered father reappears in the intimate setting of his wife's chamber. In *Hamlet*, Gertrude seems not to see the Ghost and it is possible that it is a figment of Hamlet's distraught imagination, whereas an equivalent scene in *Antonio's Revenge* threatens to topple over into farce. Maria, in her chamber, addresses an over-elaborate conceit to her 'widow bed': 'Open thy leaves, and whilst on thee I tread/ Groan out, "Alas, my dear Andrugio's dead!"' (III. iv. 62–3). This is followed by the stage direction 'MARIA *draweth the curtain, and the Ghost of* ANDRUGIO *is displayed sitting on the bed'*. There is no ambiguity in the scene as Maria accepts the Ghost's injunction to join in vengeance with Antonio. In this apparition, the supernatural element, awesome in *Hamlet*, is domesticated and treated with some bathos.

In further appearances, Andrugio's ghost is almost a participant in the revenge conspiracy; he familiarly haunts the stage, urging his son to be 'peerless in revenge', then advising him on his course of action. He is a triumphant presence in the final act, witnessing and commenting approvingly on Antonio's revenge: ''Tis done; and now my soul shall sleep in rest./ Sons that revenge their father's blood are blest' (V. v. 81–2). Andrugio's couplet conveys a sense of revenge as a duty readily executed, one that is beyond all reasonable doubt and devoid of the emotional turmoil we have seen in earlier avengers. The religious questioning of the provenance of the Ghost and its injunction to revenge, pervasive in *Hamlet*, are entirely absent in a play where revenge is represented primarily in terms of melodramatic family vendetta.

The differences in emphasis between Marston's play and earlier revenge plays can in part be related to his inclination toward satire. As a verse satirist, Marston had created characters who embodied a degenerate present of debased patronage, sexual libertinism, religious hypocrisy and economic exploitation. The issues are different in *Antonio's Revenge*, but there is a similar tendency in characters towards self-advertisement as they boast of their nefarious acts or are transparent in their motives. The idiom is brilliantly exemplified in the opening scene, as the villainous Piero Sforza, Duke of Venice, enters exultantly, barely containing his delight at the murder of his old rival Andrugio, Duke of Genoa, and of the courtier Feliche: 'I can scarce coop triumphing Vengeance up/ From bursting forth in braggart passion' (I. i. 11–12). Piero's bombast is that of the stage tyrant as he declares 'I am great in blood,/ Unequalled in revenge.' His ambitions know no bounds; vaingloriously, he projects how he will control the Italian states and 'conquer Rome' so that he can 'pop out the light of bright religion' (IV. i. 266–7). We could see here a parody of the kind of overreaching rhetoric we have seen in Chettle's *Hoffman*. The extravagance of confession and the mannerist style are, however, peculiar to Marston and evident in his other plays. In the figure of Piero there is a conscious deployment of comic bravura[4] which is similar to that employed by Mendoza, the comic villain in Marston's tragicomedy *The Malcontent*.

The distinctive theatrical idiom of *Antonio's Revenge* can also be attributed to theatrical auspices. Marston was writing for child actors, performing in an intimate, indoor space, before an audience of no more than a hundred spectators, a fraction of the size of the audience that would have seen *The Spanish Tragedy* or *Titus Andronicus*. Conditions of performance clearly shape the style, tone and emotional register of the play. The loud theatricalism of *Antonio's Revenge* is struck by the words of the gloom-laden prologue, who enlists the ideal spectator of the play:

> But if a breast
> Nailed to the earth with grief, if any heart
> Pierced through with anguish, pant within this ring,
> If there be any blood whose heat is choked
> And stifled with true sense of misery,

If ought of these strains fill this consort up,
Th'arrive most welcome.

(ll. 21-27)

Such a knowing appeal to the spectators alerts us to the nature
of the performance for which actors and audience are huddled
together in an intimate space. The overwrought imagery,
moreover, is an indication that we are not to take altogether
seriously the histrionics of the play about to be performed.
Revenge in public theatre plays like *The Spanish Tragedy* had
been associated with a profound sense of injustice, eliciting an
outraged response on the part of the protagonist. It would have
been difficult to replicate such passions on the small stage of
Paul's theatre,[5] especially when the parts were to be performed
by boys. One solution for a dramatist would be to incorporate
elements that parody the emotions and attitudes represented in
earlier plays of revenge, and this Marston seems to have done.
Antonio's Revenge exhibits a zestful theatrical self-reflexivity,
exploiting for its own ends the rhetorical laments, gestures and
declarations of revenge evident in such plays as *The Spanish
Tragedy* and *Titus Andronicus*. That boy actors with their high-
pitched voices and small stature were speaking and acting the
parts of overblown tyrants and bloodthirsty avengers may have
produced an absurdly comic tone in performance complement-
ing the often outrageous and bizarre events of the play.[6]

The term revenge is bandied around liberally in the play.
Piero glosses his outrageous actions against Andrugio, a rival in
love as well as for power, as revenge. Within the structure of
Antonio's Revenge Piero appears as the equivalent of the evil
avenger Lorenzo in *The Spanish Tragedy*, who usurps and
appropriates the term revenge to rationalize envious and
vindictive acts. Marston, however, strives for quite a different
effect, and Piero's self-declared villainy, conveyed through
language of superficial bluster, is devoid of any elaborate
intrigue and excites little psychological interest. He acknowledges immediately that he is full of 'rankling malice' and
hypocrisy towards Antonio, Andrugio's son, giving him a 'Judas
kiss' with a 'covert touch of fleering hate' (I. i. 60–61). His attack
on Strotzo, his accomplice, as he admonishes him for his
slowness in praising his diabolical ingenuity, is a tirade of comic
frenzy: 'O I could eat / Thy fumbling throat for thy lagged

59

censure' (I. i. 79–80). Then, when Strotzo is apparently at a loss for words of admiration at his treachery, his response is megalomaniac bombast: 'No! Yes! Nothing but "no" and "yes", dull lump?/ Canst thou not honey me with fluent speech/ And even adore my topless villainy?' Piero's role, in common with others, requires very little modulation of tone and feeling. When his daughter Mellida – whom he manipulates in his plot against Antonio – is reported dead, he admits freely that his grief is specious. Such superficiality of emotion seems quite deliberately an aspect of the play's melodramatic style and effect, inviting no moral response to the shallowness of human feeling.

At the end of the play when Antonio executes his grotesque revenge, there would have been cause for Piero to respond in a different register, but Marston simply pre-empts this in having the avengers mutilate him. When presented with the severed limbs of his son Julio, his distress can only be expressed through gesture: 'PIERO *seems to condole his son.*' Silenced, Piero's rant now becomes the property of the avengers. Verbal excess, whether the emotion expressed is grief, anger or vengeance, is the play's keynote and in histrionic expression there is little to distinguish the victims of crime from its perpetrators. Antonio's response to the Ghost's call from below stage for murder is conveyed in a ghoulish conceit: 'Aye, I will murder; graves and ghosts/ Fright me no more; I'll suck red vengeance/ Out of Piero's wounds, Piero's wounds' (III. ii. 77–9). Indeed, we can see here, as elsewhere, how Marston travesties or stylizes the language of earlier revenge plays. Andrugio's words to his son, 'Antonio, revenge! ... Revenge my blood', could be a parody of an early, lost version of *Hamlet* which is thought to predate Shakespeare's play. From Thomas Lodge's reference in *Wits Misery* (1596) to what has come to be referred to as the 'Ur Hamlet', we know that the Ghost 'cried so miserably at the Theatre like an oyster wife, "Hamlet, revenge"'.[7] Antonio is joined in his vengeance by the courtiers Alberto and Pandulpho. As they enact a ritual of revenge, wreathing arms, Pandulpho vows, 'We'll sit as heavy on Piero's heart,/ As Etna does on groaning Pelorus': a line which Antonio caps with 'Let's think a plot; then pell-mell vengeance' (IV. v. 92–5). 'Think a plot' and 'pell-mell' convey both the consciously theatrical and the improvisatory nature of this vengeance. Little is premeditated, nor are moral issues debated, as the headstrong, reckless revengers do their work.

The events of the play are bizarre and discontinuous. In Piero's malign deeds and in Antonio's equally violent retaliation there is some recall of the plotting and counter-plotting of *The Spanish Tragedy*, yet *Antonio's Revenge* has none of the intricate scheming of the early play. The superficial nature of the intrigue is further illustrated in Antonio's adoption of disguises, first as an Amazon and then as a fool. Such disguises evoke the role-playing and dissembling of earlier avengers; but concealment is only loosely connected to the revenge dynamic of the play and the different roles, no sooner adopted than they are abandoned, have no psychological significance. Antonio's disguise as a fool is ostensibly to enable him to remain at court and pursue vengeance, while lulling Piero into the false security of the belief that he is dead. Moreover, as Antonio tells his accomplices, the role of fool permits certain immunities, an allusion to the fool's 'licence' in freedom of speech. But such purposes are never realized and disguise seems instead to perform a metadramatic function. The stage direction reads '*Enter* ANTONIO *in a fool's habit, with a little toy of a walnut shell and soap to make bubbles*', thus drawing attention to the childishness of the actor playing the part.[8] Role-playing has very little to do with duplicity or contrivance, as it does in other revenge plays: instead, it is yet another aspect of the re-direction of the audience towards the play's aesthetics.

Antonio's first act of vengeance is the dispassionate killing of Julio, and here, quite evidently, there is recall of classical and native revenge drama. The desecration of Julio's body has resonances of the grisly revenge of Atreus in *Thyestes* and that of Titus in *Titus Andronicus*. Again, Marston seems to aim for a different effect. In the latter play, Chiron and Demetrius have committed the most atrocious crimes and within the revenge code there is a primitive justice in their treatment. In *Thyestes*, while conceptually Atreus's murder of his brother's children is no less horrible than that of Julio, the impact is muted through report by the Chorus. But in Antonio's chance encounter with Julio, his recognition of the form his revenge will take and his slow movement towards the killing of Julio – a murder that Antonio perversely represents as part of heaven's justice –

Marston arouses revulsion. In the killing of Julio, Marston has
created the one pathetic act of the play and one that is tonally
different from the play's histrionic register. Throughout the
play, Marston has shaped material to suit a particular theatrical
style designed to accommodate the limitations of his actors and
staging. It may well have been that, with a cast of boy actors,
Marston envisaged that a scene depicting the pitiful murder of a
child was within the emotional range of the player and could be
played straight.

In plays such as *The Spanish Tragedy* and *Titus Andronicus*, the
enormity of the crimes against and by the protagonists is
accompanied by an extreme sense of loss that can only be
appeased by retribution. The revenger deliberates whether or
not to act and may consider other possibilities. In *Antonio's
Revenge* no such depths of emotion or individuation of feeling
are explored; instead, the play draws attention to its rhetorical
construction in mimicking or inflating passion.[9] Characters
strike poses and affect attitudes that are then undercut by their
subsequent words or actions, and this proclivity is reinforced by
the theatrical imagery they employ. Antonio declares resolutely
to the wrongly imprisoned Mellida: 'I will not swell like a
tragedian/ In forced passion of affected strains' (II. iii. 104–5).
His subsequent reaction in lying down and weeping undermines his declaration of self-control. Pandulpho, too, initially
distances himself from player-like extremities of feeling. When
he hears of the deaths of Andrugio and his own son Feliche,
Pandulpho's restraint contrasts with Antonio's overwrought
reaction to the news. His grief appears to find an outlet in
laughter: laughter which is not, as it was with Titus in *Titus
Andronicus*, a prelude to grief, but a means of resisting grief.
Indeed, he scorns the kind of rhetorical passion we have seen in
The Spanish Tragedy and affects a stoical – and aesthetic –
distance from pain and loss: 'Why, wherefore should I weep?/
Come, sit, kind nephew; come on; thou and I/ Will talk as chorus
to this tragedy' (I. ii. 299–300). Pandulpho appears as the true
Stoic, a type that Chapman was to represent in Clermont in *The
Revenge of Bussy D'Ambois*, and the antithesis of a man like Kyd's
Hieronimo, who could be alluded to in the following lines:

> Wouldst have me cry, run raving up and down
> For my son's loss? Wouldst have me turn rank mad,

Or wring my face with mimic action,
Stamp, curse, weep, rage, and then my bosom strike?
Away, 'tis apish action, player-like.

(I. v. 76–80)

It would seem here that Marston is defining his play, its characters and its speech against a popular revenge play such as *The Spanish Tragedy* and mocking the rhetorical acting style of some public theatre plays. There is more, though, to the stage imagery than a side-swipe at Marston's commercial rivals. Pandulpho maintains his stoical stance, affirming self-restraint even when Piero orders his banishment (II. ii). However, when Piero relents momentarily and returns the body of Feliche to his father, Pandulpho's desire for revenge is ignited and there is a volte-face, appropriately enough conveyed in a theatrical metaphor: 'Man will break out, despite philosophy./ Why, all this while I ha' but played a part,/ Like to some boy that acts a tragedy' (IV. v. 46–8). The last line is yet another ironic allusion to the play's production by children, but the simile also draws attention to the way characters are defined not psychologically or through moral consciousness, but by self-fashioning. The play's characters assume a part; nothing is internalized. Pandulpho sees himself as a Stoic in the mould of Seneca, the philosopher, and ends by becoming a blood avenger of Senecan drama, as his declaration to Antonio demonstrates: 'O now, he that wants soul to kill a slave,/ Let him die slave and rot in peasant's grave' (V. iii. 66–7). Nothing is premeditated as Pandulpho and Antonio assume parts in a plot of their own improvisation.

The theatrical self-reflexivity of *Antonio's Revenge* is matched by a literary self-awareness. Marston recalls the plays of Seneca, as had his predecessors, but, whereas Kyd had used Seneca to validate his highly original drama, Marston's evocation of Seneca is rather more ironic. The characters of *Antonio's Revenge* lard their speeches with lengthy – but often subtly modified – extracts from the plays and the philosophical works. Maria, fearing for Antonio's safety and appearing in the conventional guise of the distracted woman with her hair unloosened, compares herself to Medea 'invoking all the spirits of the grave'. Yet there is nothing in the character or role of Maria which bears any resemblance to Medea. Antonio then enters and his eight-line speech in Latin is taken from Seneca's

63

Thyestes. Again, Seneca is quoted to embellish a speech rather than to suggest a structural or subconscious parallel. Later, in the same scene, Antonio encounters Julio and begins to formulate the sacrificial mode of his revenge; he applauds, surely ironically, 'bounteous heaven' for providing him with the opportunity and quotes approvingly lines in Latin from *Thyestes* which translate as 'At length has vengeance come into my power,/ And that to the full'. We could say that Antonio's identification here with Atreus and his pursuit of this grotesque revenge as a fitting closure indicates how morally reprehensible he has become. But Marston does not allow for the kind of metamorphosis we have seen in Hieronimo or Titus; there is simply very little characterization or development as such. The reiterated appropriation of Seneca is there to appeal to the educated audience of the indoor, private theatre. In drawing attention to the classical models for the rhetoric and the violent excesses of his characters' actions, Marston is not so much imitating Seneca as attempting to create a neo-Senecan drama. We could apply here the theoretical term of 'defamiliarization': that is, the audience/reader sees linguistic and dramatic conventions in a different and critical light when they are removed from their normal context. Through such devices Marston draws the audience's attention to revenge's character-istic form and his innovatory treatment of it.

Marston places *Antonio's Revenge* in a line of native and Senecan revenge plays, while subverting expectations of the tradition. Nowhere is this deconstruction of the revenge play more apparent than in the play's closure. By this time there is little to distinguish between the play's two avengers, although the Venetian senators are ready to reward Antonio and his party as 'well-seasoned props' of the state. There is, though, no elevation to power, as Marston challenges the convention of the death of the revenger – by suicide, retribution or accident – and provides the improbable, but in the play's fantastic idiom appropriate, alternative of the revenger taking up the monastic life. Yet another role is assumed by Antonio who, as the Venetian senators praise his actions, declares that the avenging faction 'will live enclosed/ In holy verge of some religious order,/ Most constant votaries' (V. vi. 34–6). That the ending is unanticipated is irrelevant: but, in dissociating tragedy and revenge, Marston has given a further bold twist to the revenge play.

THE REVENGER'S TRAGEDY

The Revenger's Tragedy is now thought to have been written by Thomas Middleton, and not, as was earlier supposed, by Cyril Tourneur.[10] Middleton, like Marston, wrote for Paul's Boys, yet *The Revenger's Tragedy* was performed by the King's Men at the Globe theatre in the early Jacobean period. Although produced by the leading adult players for the open air, public theatre, in common with *Antonio's Revenge* the play self-consciously deploys and parodies conventions and motifs associated with revenge plays. However, in evoking scenes from earlier plays, particularly *Hamlet*, *The Revenger's Tragedy* can be seen in relation to a theatrical tradition of revenge rather than to a literary one. Notably, there is no use of Senecan rhetoric or recall of classical precedent as there is in other revenge drama. Instead, *The Revenger's Tragedy* evinces a heightened sense of theatricality demonstrable in the repeated use of the aside and a delight in role-playing, disguise and intrigue. Most of the characters are dissemblers, hiding their motives and feigning friendship to exploit others. Indeed the play's salient theatrical features are symptomatic of an all-pervasive duplicity in the enclosed world of the Italian court that Middleton has created. The play's distinctiveness is conveyed in its non-rhetorical idiom: in its mixture of informal, colloquial, often ironic dialogue and the lyrical, sometimes feverish, verse uttered by Vindici, the revenge protagonist, when he is brooding on or anatomizing the decadence and corruption of the Italianate court.

Whereas Thomas Kyd had, in the chorus of *The Spanish Tragedy*, personified revenge outside the play, Middleton embodies it in his central character, Vindici. As his name suggests, he is the play's *raison d'être*. In pursuing vengeance for the murder by the Duke of his lover Gloriana, Vindici delights in concealing his role from those he is plotting to destroy. When the Duke's son Lussurioso (translatable as 'the lascivious one'), in hiring his services, asks him his name, there is conscious irony in Vindici's replies:

LUSSURIOSO. Thy name, I have forgot it
VINDICI. Vindici, my lord.
LUSSURIOSO. 'Tis a good name, that.
VINDICI. Ay, a revenger.
LUSSURIOSO. It does betoken courage; thou shouldst be valiant,
    And kill thine enemies.
VINDICI. That's my hope, my lord.

(IV. ii. 176–9)

Vindici's mordant delight in ambiguity is matched by his enthusiasm for changing identity. The professed purpose of Vindici's disguise is to infiltrate and destroy the ducal family, and to these ends Hippolito, his brother and accomplice, introduces him, in the guise of Piato, a courtier on the make, to Lussurioso. This leads to one of several moments of black farce as Lussurioso later hires Vindici in his proper person to murder his alter ego, Piato. Vindici switches with ease from one role to another, at times in danger of forgetting the role he is playing. As a pimp, he plays the part with notable relish and, after rationalizing away his initial doubts, he acts the tempter and seducer to his own sister (Fig. 6). He can enjoy, in his disguise, putting aside the incest taboo and when Castiza spiritedly rejects his temptations, he rejoices in his sister's chastity. In contrast with earlier avengers, there is with Vindici very little sense of identity, either social or psychological. Like an accomplished actor, Vindici becomes the part he is playing; if he discloses little of himself outside the part, that is because there is nothing to disclose.

There is no moral ambiguity or self-doubt in Vindici's thoughts and no wavering over the legitimacy of revenge, as there is in the cases of Hieronimo, Titus and Hamlet. Vindici's set purpose is conveyed in his opening soliloquy when he reveals in satirical and sardonic tone the corruption of the court that is personified in the figure of the Duke and his extended family. There is no prospect of justice: the Duke is the law and is himself beyond its reach, and in this situation Vindici can only redress the imbalance between his sense of natural justice and the murder of Gloriana by appointing himself judge and executioner. Yet there is modulation of tone in the soliloquy. As he addresses the skull of Gloriana (Fig. 7), a striking and literal use of a relic of remembrance, his words are haunted and haunting:

Figure 6. Antony Sher as Vindici and Stella Gonet as Castiza in the 1987 Royal Shakespeare production of *The Revenger's Tragedy*, directed by Di Trevis. Joe Cocks Studio Collection © Shakespeare Birthplace Trust.

Figure 7. Antony Sher as Vindici in the 1987 Royal Shakespeare Company production of *The Revenger's Tragedy*, directed by Di Trevis. Joe Cocks Studio Collection © Shakespeare Birthplace Trust.

> Thou sallow picture of my poisoned love,
> My study's ornament, thou shell of death,
> Once the bright face of my betrothed lady,
> - When life and beauty naturally filled out
> These ragged imperfections.

(I. i. 14–18)

Nine years have elapsed since the poisoning of Gloriana and after such an interval it may seem somewhat absurd for Vindici to declare that murder never escapes vengeance: 'Who e'er knew/ Murder unpaid? Faith, give Revenge her due/ She has kept touch hitherto.' Vindici has been waiting, we are led to believe, for the perfect opportunity to enter inner court circles and destroy not only the Duke, but the entire line of succession. Nine years, it has been pointed out, is the time it takes for the flesh to rot from Gloriana's skull, enabling it to function as both *memento mori* and – stripped of flesh – a symbol of purity (lost when it is attired).[11] This intensifies the moral symbolism of the skull, but, just as significant, is how the sense of lapsed time intensifies the image of the revenger's fixity of purpose. As he anticipates his first act of revenge, Vindici distils this long wait into one moment of exquisite pleasure: 'Now nine years' vengeance crowd into a minute.' Vindici inflicts a terrible death on the Duke, punishing him for all his sins in a way that fits them, with a sadistic delight fuelled by grief and outrage.

No sooner is the Duke dead than Vindici gleefully declares his plan to exterminate the Duke's successors: 'As fast as they peep up, let's cut 'em down.' In contrast with earlier plays, revenge becomes largely an end in itself or at best a ritual cleansing of society's corruption, as is conveyed by Vindici's moralizing commentary at strategic moments in the play. Once he has poisoned the Duke, he declares, 'When the bad bleeds, then is the tragedy good' (III. v. 199). Lussurioso, as corrupt as his father, is Vindici's next victim, and he dies to the sound of thunder while Vindici alludes to divine approval of his act: 'No power is angry when the lustful die/ When thunder claps, heaven likes the tragedy' (V. iii. 48–9). His sense of the moral rectitude of his role is, of course, his undoing, as, not satisfied with ensuring that his victims identify him, he incriminates himself in disclosing the part he has played in the murderous havoc of the final scene. He remonstrates with his brother that

69

death is no great matter now that the task is complete: 'Are we not revenged?/ Is there one enemy left alive amongst those?/ 'Tis time to die, when we are ourselves our foes' (V. iii. 107–9). This easy acceptance of death coupled with his jubilant acknowledgement of his revenging role hardly fits certain preconceptions of tragedy. In dramatic effect nothing could be further from the close of *Hamlet*. There is no sense of catharsis or loss in *The Revenger's Tragedy*. Vindici's consummate identification with his role is far removed from Hamlet's dying concern with his wounded name and reputation. Vindici knows that he has played his part to perfection and therein lies his satisfaction.

Revenge, for Vindici, does entail justice, but much more, it becomes an art as Vindici seeks a particular kind of revenge which is sadistically appropriate to satisfy dark, unacknowledged urges within him. The Duke's death is grotesquely witty: he kisses the poisoned, masked skull of Gloriana, believing it to be a country woman (Fig. 8) and, in the throes of death, he becomes a voyeur as he is made to witness his Duchess seduce his bastard son Spurio. There is an additional level of irony in that Spurio regards his seduction by the Duchess as revenge against his father for his illegitimate conception and so there is a double vengeance enacted in the scene. As revenge becomes an end in itself and Vindici loses himself in its aesthetics, the original motive for that revenge becomes almost incidental. Vindici himself, in his exchange with Hippolito as they prepare to poison the Duke, seems dimly aware of this. In a scene reminiscent of the graveyard scene in *Hamlet*, he ponders his own love for Gloriana – although he never uses her name – and, gazing at the skull, wonders at his own obsessions: 'And now methinks I could e'en chide myself/ For doting on her beauty, though her death/ Shall be revenged after no common action' (III. v. 68–70). However, he stops short of acknowledging the futility of revenge and retains to the end the sense of rightness that compels his actions and makes him confess them. He is true to his word that his vengeance is 'no common action': in the perverse nature of the revenge he has planned, he treats Gloriana as a ventriloquist does his dummy (III. v. 43–8) and makes her his accomplice, figuratively bearing a part in her own revenge. Vindici's revenge is driven by the same obsessions and compulsions as earlier avengers and he attains a similar sense of

Figure 8. David Waller as the Duke and Ian Richardson as Vindici in the 1966 Royal Shakespeare Company production of *The Revenger's Tragedy*, directed by Trevor Nunn. Photographer Reg Wilson © Royal Shakespeare Company.

liberation through retribution, but there is no theatrical precedent for his witty and cruel retributive strategy.[12]

The Revenger's Tragedy goes beyond any earlier revenge play in depicting a society in which general human depravity is endemic. The world of the play is peopled by extravagant stereotypes of vice and occasional virtue, with such traits distributed according to rank. Vice is an aristocratic prerogative. The Duke and heirs express their wealth and power almost exclusively through the language of sexual coercion; murder and rape are their stock in trade. Whereas in *Hamlet* the sense of corruption in Elsinore is mainly filtered through Hamlet's consciousness, in *The Revenger's Tragedy* Vindici's dark vision is endorsed by all that is said and performed. The characters are remarkably candid about themselves and do not seek to justify their degeneracy beyond stating that this is how they are. In psychoanalytical terms they are ruled by the id, the dark inaccessible part of the personality, striving for satisfaction of instinctual needs and knowing no value judgement or morality.[13] The ducal family are blind to circumstance, seeing only their own wish-world. Spurio succumbs with the flimsiest of excuses to the sexual advances of his stepmother: 'Duke, thou didst do me wrong, and by thy act/ Adultery is my nature' (I. iii. 176–7). When the Duchess's son is imprisoned for the rape of the old lord Antonio's wife, he thinks only of further gratification: 'Well then, 'tis done, and it would please me well/ Were it to do again' (I. ii. 60–61). In his short soliloquy at the close of the second act, spoken as he has pardoned Lussurioso, the Duke freely admits his own guilt and the corollary that, as a guilty judge, he should ignore the crimes of others:

> It well becomes that judge to nod at crimes,
> That does commit greater himself, and lives.
> I may forgive a disobedient error
> That expect pardon for adultery
> And in my old days am a youth in lust!
> Many a beauty have I turned to poison
> In the denial, covetous of all.
> Age hot is like a monster to be seen:
> My hairs are white, and yet my sins are green

> (II. iii. 124–32)

We could compare this soliloquy, which is in fact more like an aside, to that of Claudius in *Hamlet*, when in prayer he admits to the murder of his brother. Claudius reveals a sense of conscience, but realizes that he cannot expect any divine pardon when he is unable to relinquish the prizes of his villainy. The Duke's sense of sin contains no such doubt: he acknowledges unspecified crimes and he assumes that pardon – divine or human, it is not clear – will be granted.

All the members of the court act with a similar disregard for personal accountability. Vindici, acting in his role as pander, remarks to Lussurioso that all manner of sin will go undetected, but then slips in a veiled warning: 'save the eternal eye/ That sees through flesh and all'. Lussurioso is not discomforted, declaring that sin is innate: 'It is our blood to err, though hell gaped loud.' In the masque to commemorate his accession to the dukedom, however, he is alarmed by the sudden appearance of a blazing star and is aware of its ominous significance. This belated fear of a reckoning would seem to be consistent with Vindici's moralistic allusions to a belief in the role of providence. How seriously we are to take these pieties is open to question. The peals of thunder which are heard as Vindici plots and enacts his revenge are interpreted by him as expressions of divine approval: 'Mark thunder! Dost know thy cue, thou big-voiced cryer.' Yet the language of his address, in its scant deference to providence, undercuts any sense of awe, and it is possible, as Jonathan Dollimore has argued, that in performance this may have come across as a comic allusion to an outmoded stage convention.[14] When Vindici is incredulous at Lussurioso's cool villainy, he wonders 'that such a fellow, impudent and wicked/ Should not be cloven as he stood'. In answer to his question 'Is there no thunder left?', thunder is heard. In the 1987 Royal Shakespeare Company production, Vindici's call to the heavens was accompanied by throttled laughter. If Vindici is directing his audience to laugh at old-fashioned theatrical effects and the attendant invocation of divine wrath, this would be consistent with the play's metatheatricality. A mocking of providential intervention does not exclude a secular gratification when at last the villains get their come-uppance.

If from our twenty-first-century post-Freudian perspective, it is possible to see the characters in terms of the id uncontrolled by the ego, the response of the play's original audience might well have been shaped by another set of cultural assumptions. In their extravagant, non-individualized nastiness, members of the ducal court could be said to represent the vices of the medieval morality play.[15] Indeed, the opening torch-lit scene, in which the Duke and his extended family process across the stage, is like a dumb show in which are represented the deadly sins of moral allegory. At one level they are grotesque caricatures of pride, lust, gluttony and ambition, as their very names – Lussurioso, Supervacuo, Ambitioso, Spurio – suggest. Within such a morality play structure Vindici, as social outsider, is both repelled and fascinated by the lusts and desires he attacks. His mood swings from a vigorous condemnation of vice to an almost joyous participation in the intrigues of court. He laments Gloriana, but, typical of the malcontent's pathology, he is a misogynist: 'Wives are but made to go to bed and feed' is the aside he mutters against his mother. Yet it is not Vindici but his sister Castiza who, by her opposition to the sexual tyranny of Lussurioso, offers the play some moral relief.

The theatrical qualities of *The Revenger's Tragedy* have been captured in several notable productions in the later twentieth century. The first RSC production, in 1966, on the main stage was visually splendid with characters dressed in black and silver. Vindici, played by Ian Richardson, was a cool, sadistic executioner, bitter and ironic. The RSC again staged the play in 1987, this time in the smaller Swan theatre with its apron stage.[16] The characters were luridly represented as grotesque caricatures of venality dressed in heavy brocade costumes and outlandish wigs. The actors' faces were made up with florid cheeks and red-rimmed eyes. The central stage image was a ramp that doubled as a bed and a scaffold. The livid decadence of a court that is alluded to by Vindici as 'wildfire at midnight' was conveyed by rows of candles behind the arras. Antony Sher as Vindici, first emerging from a stage trap clutching Gloriana's skull, was a psychopath pursuing an obsession, expressing a terrible, violent joy at his revenge. His unkempt appearance and manic fixity of purpose reflected Bacon's maxim that 'a man that studieth revenge keeps his wounds green': nine years' brooding and dwelling constantly on this life-destroying experience had reduced Vindici to a beggarly malcontent, a disorderly hermit.

However, through role-playing, this Vindici acquired a new vibrancy, conveying both an energetic sense of malignity as he pursued his revenge and a ferocious logic in his quest for moral justice.

As several productions of the play suggest, there is much in the eclectic style of *The Revenger's Tragedy* that appeals to postmodern sensibility. The play trades on irony and black comedy, while employing haunting *memento mori* visual and verbal imagery. Demotic speech vies with terse and vivid poetic imagery. It is a play which is highly conscious of its theatricality. Yet disguise and role playing are symptomatic not of the play's aesthetics, as in *Antonio's Revenge*, but of duplicity and the opacity characters strive for in their relation to others. Similarly, the playfulness of *The Revenger's Tragedy* does not extend to the notion of revenge itself. There are touches of farce and mordant humour in Vindici's ingenuity as he plots against and destroys the ducal family. Yet no play exposes in quite the same way the obsessive nature of revenge and how it maims those who use its weapons.

3

Theatre of God's Judgement

The two plays discussed in this chapter, Cyril Tourneur's *The Atheist's Tragedy* and Thomas Middleton's *The Changeling*, would seem to have very little in common in terms of both dramatic preoccupation and style. Middleton's play is by far the better known and has received a good deal more critical attention. The reasons for this are not difficult to deduce. In the partnership of Beatrice Joanna and De Flores in *The Changeling* there is an extraordinary psychological intensity which makes the relationships of *The Atheist's Tragedy* appear flat and formulaic in comparison. What suggests bringing these plays together is that in refracting the idea of revenge as providential, bound up with the Old Testament ethos of God's wrath against the unrighteous, the two plays are similarly framed by a concept of divine retribution. In *The Revenger's Tragedy*, Vindici had alluded to the all-seeing eye of providence, yet the play's outlook is essentially secular. In neither *The Atheist's Tragedy* nor *The Changeling* is there an active agent of vengeance. Instead, in the nemesis of both plays, providence is represented as the determinative factor in the strict calling to account projected in the plays' final moments. Human revenge is resisted – in *The Changeling* more by default – so that redress of wrongs and the exposure of murder are identified on stage with the providential ideology evident in such works as Thomas Beard's *The Theatre of God's Judgements* (1597) and John Reynolds's *The Triumphs of God's Revenge Against the Crying and Execrable Sin of Murder* (1621).

In form and texture the plays are similarly constructed in that they both reveal the instability of revenge as a tragic form. The dramatic realization of the visitation of God's vengeance on the wicked, a central tenet of Puritanism, might seem to constitute sombre, homiletic theatre. Yet *The Atheist's Tragedy* and *The*

Changeling challenge such decorum, juxtaposing farcical and comic scenes with others projecting images of sin and human self-destruction. The unmediated changes from semi-naturalistic to non-naturalistic modes of theatrical expression have an unsettling effect on the audience. In responding to the totality of the drama we have to interpret the interaction of the play's disparate idioms.

THE ATHEIST'S TRAGEDY OR THE HONEST MAN'S REVENGE

Comparatively little is known of Cyril Tourneur, the author of *The Atheist's Tragedy*, or of the play's auspices. Tourneur wrote various non-dramatic works, including verse satire and elegy, while professionally serving as secretary to Sir Francis Vere, commander of Elizabeth I's forces in the Netherlands. It is not a coincidence that Charlemont in *The Atheist's Tragedy* fights at the Siege of Ostend, a campaign with which Tourneur would have been familiar.[1] For most of the twentieth century it was accepted that both *The Revenger's Tragedy* and *The Atheist's Tragedy* were the work of Tourneur. It is of course possible, as Shakespeare had demonstrated in *Titus Andronicus* and *Hamlet*, for a dramatist to produce plays with starkly different representations and explorations of revenge. But the language, style and theatrical idiom of *The Revenger's Tragedy* and *The Atheist's Tragedy* are so individually distinctive that it is hard to believe that they were produced by the same playwright.

In scenic form and in language there are resonances in *The Atheist's Tragedy* of earlier revenge plays; like *Hamlet*, *Hoffman* and *Antonio's Revenge*, it is a play about the response of a son to the murder of a father. The apparition of the Ghost in *The Atheist's Tragedy* (II .vi.) evokes the encounter of the Ghost of Old Hamlet with the sentries on the battlements. Specifically, the opening dialogue between Charlemont and the sergeant is reminiscent of the unease felt by Barnardo Marcellus, and Francisco before the appearance of the Ghost, while the ending of the scene, when the musketeer challenges the apparition and fires his musket, evokes Marcellus's aborted attempt to strike the Ghost with his spear. If the former scene in *The Atheist's Tragedy* consciously draws on the opening scene in *Hamlet*, it also radically departs from it. There is a more obvious melodramatic effect in the entry of Montferrers's Ghost, portended as it is by thunder and lightning, and, when the father does address the son, his message to exercise restraint in revenge is very different from the injunction of Old Hamlet. At other moments in the play, Tourneur seems to be inverting motifs evident in *Hamlet*. When D'Amville returns to France to find that Castabella is married to D'Amville's son Sebastian, he accuses her of female inconstancy in language reminiscent of Hamlet's misogynist response to Gertrude and Ophelia. But this is a temporary aberration on Charlemont's part, as he accepts that Castabella was forced into the marriage. Castabella's loyalty is vindicated and, unlike the destruction of Hamlet's relationship with Ophelia, the love of Charlemont and Castabella survives the test. The formal relationship between the two plays is superficial. There is a predictable moderation of tragic effect in *The Atheist's Tragedy* as the typical drive of the revenge play towards redress of wrong by human agency – and the attendant havoc – is averted and Charlemont is exempted from the mental pressures induced by the duty of revenge that Hamlet has to endure.

The same reworking of motifs in *The Atheist's Tragedy* can be seen in relation to *The Revenger's Tragedy*. In the latter play the sound of thunder, conventionally signifying divine approval or disapproval, can be interpreted as stage parody. In *The Atheist's Tragedy*, however, where providence emerges as dictating the pattern of revenge, an audience is expected to take the thunder more literally. D'Amville, who, like Claudius in *Hamlet*, murders his brother to gain power, is a professed 'atheist'. Within the play this is a term which is synonymous with amorality and materiality rather than simply an ideology which rejects a theistic belief. As D'Amville and his accomplice Borachio gloatingly rehearse their success in the murder of Montferrers, D'Amville dismisses any notion of divine omnipresence: 'Here was a murder bravely carried through/ The eye of observation, unobserved' (II. iv. 134–5). The defiant anti-providential speech is interrupted and undercut by thunder and lightning, which D'Amville dismisses as due to natural causes. From rejecting the notion of an all-seeing deity, and instead invoking Nature[2] as a substitute presence, D'Amville argues that first Nature 'winked at our proceedings' and, then, according to D'Amville's reading of the thunder, favoured the 'performance'. The use of the acting term 'performance' to denote murder is characteristic of the atheist's outlook – in which aesthetics replace ethics – and indicative of the way he feigns and improvises feeling. More significant is the atheist's opportunistic reading of the signs: Nature 'favoured our performance' and 'winked at our proceedings' (II. iv. 157–64). In the speech, Nature is seen to turn a blind eye to murder and – more actively – to encourage it. The atheist's blatant appropriation of the thunder to endorse murder suggests that the audience respond conventionally to its peals. Thunder is no extra-textual device to heighten the revenge theme as it is in the opening scene of *Hoffman* or the Pyrrhus speech in *Hamlet* (II. ii. 482), but would seem to denote the fallacy of D'Amville's material outlook. What appears to be a theatrical parody in *The Revenger's Tragedy* of a stock-in-trade device to convey divine wrath is effectively reinstated as dramatic symbolism in a later play.

It is possible to respond to *The Atheist's Tragedy* as a rather static, mechanically conceived revenge drama. The play is structured on a philosophical material/spiritual dialectic represented by D'Amville, on one hand, and Montferrers and his son Charlemont on the other.[3] Consistent with his reiterated statement of materialist philosophy, D'Amville acts in a manner free of social, religious or moral constraint. There is the same ego tyranny we have seen in other villains in revenge plays; self-gratification is his only dictum, as he tells Borachio: 'Let all men lose, so I increase my gain:/ I have no feeling of another's pain' (I. ii. 128–9). The play's orthodox defeat of D'Amville's materialist outlook is unequivocally asserted in the final scaffold scene: in his efforts to become his nephew's executioner D'Amville destroys himself by striking out his own brains. In an ironic and punning exchange with the judge on the scaffold, the atheist, implicitly repudiating all his earlier materialist assertions, sees the hand of providence as guiding the axe:

> D'AMVILLE. What murderer was he
> That lifted up my hand against my head?
> JUDGE. None but yourself, my lord.
> D'AMVILLE.   I thought he was
> A murderer that did it.

JUDGE.   God forbid
D'AMVILLE. Forbid? You lie, judge; he commanded it

(V. ii. 241–5)

The loaded exchange offers a variation of the gallows humour we have seen in *The Spanish Tragedy* where the criminal jests with his hangman, albeit in the latter play expecting a reprieve. In *The Atheist's Tragedy* the tone is not that of black comedy, nor is it ironic or stoical; underneath the punning is a pious recognition of the play's providential stance, expressed through the character who has hitherto denied it.

As the play's title suggests, it is D'Amville and his irreligious plotting that give the play its dynamic and dramatic focus. D'Amville does not slip in and out of roles or strike up a confessional relationship with the audience; his treachery, nevertheless, involves feigning emotions and specious arguments that identify him with stage villains like Richard III, or Iago in *Othello* and Edmund in *King Lear*. As with them, there is zest in the way he dissembles emotion. D'Amville's reaction to Montferrers's death, which he has engineered, is typical. Servants enter with the body and D'Amville's baroque conceit, 'Dead be your tongues! Drop out/ Mine eye-balls, and let envious Fortune play/ At tennis with 'em' (II. iv. 27–8), enhances and adds a comic note to the display of hypocritical grief. In a play that confounds expectations of revenge tragedy, it is interesting that in *The Atheist's Tragedy* it is not, as in earlier plays, the revenger who – out of necessity – dissembles, but his opponent. Indeed, Charlemont is so taken in by his uncle's deceptions, that following the Ghost's first appearance, he considers it to be an illusion and muses on how his father could be dead when he had been left 'i' the kind regard/ Of a most loving uncle' (II. vi. 42–3). Clearly, Charlemont has none of the initial suspicion of, and aversion towards, his uncle that Hamlet strongly registers, and there is a psychologically uncomplicated transition from his trust of D'Amville to being convinced of his villainy.

The dynamics and structure of *The Atheist's Tragedy* are quite different from those of other revenge plays and there is a consequent reconfiguration of the revenger's role. The subtitle 'The Honest Man's Revenge' alerts us to a dramatic narrative which is less compelling than that of D'Amville's self-advancing actions. Following the murder of his father, it is Charlemont whom we might expect to assume the role of revenger, but the play defies expectations of the pattern of revenge drama and the would-be avenger is deprived of agency. Charlemont receives no injunctions to act and he betrays few signs of the obsessions and compulsions that drive earlier protagonists. When the Ghost of Montferrers does appear to Charlemont, who is away from France fighting in Ostend, and tells him of his murder and of Charlemont's disinheritance (II. vi), there is an undermining of expectation. Montferrers expresses an orthodox anti-revenge ethos, instructing his son to do nothing: 'Attend with patience the success of things/ But leave revenge unto the king of kings' (II. vi. 22–3). As we have seen in other avengers, to await patiently the opportunity to ensnare opponents is part of the course of revenge, but the patience that Charlemont is enjoined to exercise leaves him without any control over events. When he considers the weight of wrong against him, such patience, as he acknowledges in one of his soliloquies (III. i. 144–7) seems beyond endurance. Later, when Charlemont is about to kill D'Amville's son Sebastian, the Ghost of Montferrers appears and restrains him, invoking again the role of providence: 'Let Him revenge my murder and thy wrongs/ To whom the justice of revenge belongs' (III. ii. 32–3). Compared with the inner torment of earlier avengers, the dilemma that this injunction produces is articulated succinctly and in rational terms: 'You torture me between the passion of/ My blood, and the Religion of my soul.' Charlemont voices the classic conflict between a religious morality forbidding revenge and his own emotional need to requite his father's death. *The Atheist's Tragedy* does not venture much beyond the articulating of the dilemma. Charlemont's sense of loss is never fully felt; neither does the play expose any inner division or suggest the effect of such repression on the protagonist. Charlemont obeys his father and there is little suggestion that he suffers inwardly through the need to hold back his vengeful instincts. To an extent Tourneur would seem to have written the one thesis revenge play of the Renaissance stage. Earthly justice may, as in other plays, be unreliable and suspect, but divine justice will in the end ensure retribution. Dramatic closure comes when the ways of providence are unveiled in the serio-comic events on the scaffold. The wrongdoer perishes without the wronged individual risking his life and mental wellbeing in the cause of justice, and there are no victims.

The play's moral meaning may be unambiguous and orthodox, but it is embedded in a dramatic form and idiom which are hybrid and elusive. Scenes of absurd comedy are interspersed with philosophical meditation. If 'the king of kings' is active in the revenge of Montferrers, as his ghost maintains, he has a bizarre sense of humour. A strangely comical sequence of events precedes the final scaffold scene in which D'Amville blows out his own brains. Leading to this dénouement is a protracted graveyard scene, in which the charnel house becomes more than a motif of mortality. Charlemont piously defines the place as one conducive to spiritual meditation and his speculations on the lives of the dead clearly recall Hamlet's reminiscences of Yorick as Ophelia's grave is dug. In *The Atheist's Tragedy*, however, the graveyard, far from representing a contemplative locus, becomes a place where characters meet to have sexual intercourse, willingly or under coercion. The charlatan chaplain Languebeau Snuffe has an assignation with Soquette, servant to the wigmaker Cataplasma, for which he dons a sheet and a beard in order to pass as the Ghost of Montferrers, should they be discovered: 'This disguise is for security sake ... Now if any stranger fall upon us before our business be ended, in this disguise I shall be taken for that ghost and never be called to examination' (IV. iii. 58–62). In a sense, Snuffe's absurd impersonation of Montferrers punctures the authority of the Ghost and his ethical injunctions. How can the audience take the Ghost entirely seriously when he undergoes the comic impersonation of the sheet and the false beard?

Serious and playful elements are again entwined when Charlemont comes upon Snuffe and Soquette and they flee, leaving behind the beard, which Charlemont then wears as a disguise to protect himself. Unwittingly he assumes the persona of his dead father. D'Amville, who is also in the graveyard about to rape his daughter-in-law, is startled by the appearance of Charlemont incognito. Taking him for Montferrers, despite all his earlier rational rejections of the supernatural, he flees the churchyard in terror. Languebeau Snuffe then returns to the scene in search of Soquette and mistakes the body of Borachio, D'Amville's sidekick, who has been killed by Charlemont, for that of Soquette. Snuffe embraces the corpse and graveyard lust becomes a travesty of necrophilia:

> Verily thou liest in a fine premeditate readiness for the purpose. Come, kiss me, sweet Soquette. [*Kisses the body*] Now purity defend me from the sin of Sodom. This is a creature of the masculine gender. [*Touches the body*] Verily the man is blasted. Yea, cold and stiff! – Murder, murder, murder! (IV. iii. 206–10)

The black comedy is similar to the effect created by the Duke's tryst with the skeletal Gloriana in *The Revenger's Tragedy*, in that both men think they are embracing or about to embrace a living, sexually responsive woman. The accidental, rather than contrived, nature of this coupling of living and dead bodies gives the scene a farcical aspect not present in Vindici's ghoulish revenge. Yet both scenes provoke the same kind of uneasy laughter in the gruesome juxtaposition of sex and death.

The blending of serious, comical and grotesque idioms in the graveyard scene has been discussed in some detail because, in considering the intellectual frame of *The Atheist's Tragedy* and its illustration of a revenge thesis play, the different registers and the play's comic excesses might be ignored.[4] The subsidiary plot, which manages to be both comic in its intrigue and mistaken identities and alarming in its sexual exploitation, sets up a contrast with the chaste love affair of Charlemont and Castabella and to some extent unsettles the stoic philosophy of the play. *The Atheist's Tragedy* does endorse the implication of its subtitle. Charlemont is spared the emotional and psychological demands and the moral compromises that revenge can inflict upon the individual and he can thus remain an 'honest man'. He does receive justice for his father's death without further loss of life. In the bizarre turn of final events on the scaffold, retribution can be interpreted as part of God's purpose. Yet we might be tempted not to accept unequivocally the providential and pious ethic of the play. There is little solemnity in the last-minute providential intervention and the farcical moments of the drama leading up to the scaffold scene tend to divert attention from its more serious articulations.

In the fantastic death of D'Amville, Tourneur draws on heightened and admonitory accounts of the fates of atheistic individuals. Thomas Beard had, for example, described the death of the Elizabethan playwright Christopher Marlowe, an alleged 'atheist', as the work of providence, manifested as self-destruction:

> It so fell out that in London streets as he [Marlowe] purposed to stab one whom he sought a grudge unto with his dagger, the other party perceiving so avoided the stroke, that withall catching hold of his wrist, he stabbed his own dagger into his own head, ... The manner of his death being so terrible (for he even cursed and blasphemed to his last gasp, and together with his breath an oath flew out of his mouth) that it was not only a manifest figure of God's judgement, but also an horrible and fearful terror to all that beheld him. But herein did the justice of God most notably appear, in that he compelled his own hand which had written those blasphemies to be the instrument to punish him, and that in his brain, which had devised the same.[5]

There is an arresting parallel here in that D'Amville, like Marlowe, by bizarre accident turns his weapon away from the intended victim upon himself. The death of D'Amville does not have the same symbolic reference as Beard gives to that of Marlowe, but, allowing for the difference of genre, it is clearly part of the same ideological discourse. Beard extracts from his account of Marlowe's death the moral that it should be seen as a warning to all atheists. D'Amville takes on the role of interpretative narrator and, in his dying speech, recognizes 'the judgement I deserved'. Does the play then endorse revenge as integral to providentialism? Jonathan Dollimore has commented that providentialism in *The Atheist's Tragedy* should be regarded as a fictive category, like poetic justice, and that the comedic closure undermines the 'tragic-didactic status of providentialism'.[6] As the discussion in this chapter illustrates, the play's hybrid idiom does to some extent alert an audience to see more than a simple validation of the kind of belief expounded in Beard's work. Yet, unlike poetic justice, providentialism was a belief resolutely held by many and in *The Atheist's Tragedy* it would seem to be endorsed not only by the characters, but by the play itself. As a revenge play, *The Atheist's Tragedy* quite consciously deviates from almost all other plays examined in that it is constructed and confined within the providential frame and this frame remains unshaken by the compulsive, unruly energies of a private avenger.

THE CHANGELING

The Changeling is a collaborative work by Thomas Middleton and William Rowley. As with *The Atheist's Tragedy*, the play embodies contrasting tones and styles. In *The Changeling*, however, there is a much clearer demarcation of plot and attendant idiom: the main, tragic plot depicts murder and retribution, while the secondary plot, set in the madhouse managed by the jealous doctor Alibius, is one of comic intrigue and deception. In the dominant dramatic narrative the language is poetic, at times quite complex, and embodies startlingly compressed and psychologically insightful imagery, while the comic scenes carry a similar allusiveness in a more colloquial idiom.[7] This intertwining of disparate dramatic material has been assumed to be the result of the collaboration between the two playwrights, with editors breaking down the parts of the play and ascribing the two central dramatic scenes between Beatrice Joanna and De Flores (II. ii and III. iv) to Middleton and much of the comic subplot to Rowley. Yet, since the influential study of the play's structure by William Empson, it has also been recognized that the two dramatic narratives are integral – strategically and metaphorically related.[8] Main and subsidiary plots are brought together at the end of the fourth act when inmates from the madhouse dance at the wedding celebrations of Beatrice Joanna and Alsemero. The dance of madmen and fools serves as commentary on the main narrative; such an anarchic performance seems appropriate entertainment for a marriage facilitated by murder. Further, the Renaissance trope of love as a form of madness encompasses the different narrative strands of the play. Antonio and Franciscus enter the madhouse in pursuit of Alibius's wife and pass themselves off as two of its inmates. While the mad folk of the institution are assumed to have been robbed of their reason by nature, the characters of the main plot are deprived of rational judgement by sexual passion and recklessness. The various disguises adopted by the actors in the subplot contrast with the transformation in Beatrice Joanna brought about by passion. The drastic transformations of character which are endemic to the play are moralistically summed up in the choric comments at the end and earn the play its title.

Middleton constructs the main plot of his play from one of the stories or 'histories' in John Reynolds's admonitory collection *The Triumphs of God's Revenge Against the Crying and Execrable Sin of Murder*. In thirty 'tragical histories' originating from 'divers countries beyond the seas', Reynolds rehearsed and exemplified his theme that the hand of providence will ensure that murder will be exposed and that perpetrators will be duly punished. Scriptural authority is quoted throughout. As epigraph for the volume, Reynolds cited Psalm 9, verse 16: 'The Lord is known in executing judgement, and the wicked is snared in the work of his own hand', and this sense of inherent self-destruction is embodied in the various narratives. The fourth of the 'tragical histories' tells the story of Beatrice Joanna who, in order to marry Alsemero, 'instantly ravished and vanquished' by her, prompted De Flores to murder her former suitor Alonzo Piracquo. Middleton omits in the plot of *The Changeling* Alsemero's subsequent murder of De Flores and Beatrice Joanna when he discovers their adulterous relationship. More interestingly, the play develops the psychology of Beatrice's initial revulsion towards De Flores that develops into dependence and sexual attraction. Reynolds's story, on the other hand, follows its own logic of retribution. Alonzo's brother Tomazo, believing Alsemero to be in some way guilty of his brother's death, challenges him to a duel. He is killed and Alsemero flees Alicante; but, comments the narrator, it is 'in vain; for the justice of the Lord will both stop his horse, and arrest him'. Alsemero is indeed captured and, after divulging the part played by Beatrice and De Flores in the murder of Alonzo Piracquo, is executed. Reynolds's story glosses the motivations of the major characters almost solely in terms of revenge. Beatrice, 'boiling still in her revenge to [Alonzo] Piracquo', conspires to have him murdered; Alsemero vows that he will be revenged on Beatrice; Tomazo Piracquo desires to be revenged on Alsemero. There is no attempt to invoke the law to obtain justice; instead, revenge is an intensely personal affair, bound up as it is with desire, hatred and jealousy.

The Changeling departs from *The Triumphs of God's Revenge* in some narrative detail, but the drama is essentially constructed to suggest to the survivors and audience the workings of providence. Initially, however, there are signs that secular revenge will ensure retributive justice. When Alonzo's mysterious disappearance is made known, his brother Tomazo, suspecting foul play, assumes the mantle of revenger. As a would-be revenger Tomazo is, however, ineffectual, his ignorance of the identity of his brother's murderer adding a layer of irony to certain scenes. There is no proof of Alonzo's death, as his body has not been found, but Tomazo is quick to assume the complicity of Beatrice's father and – as the beneficiary of Alonzo's disappearance – her new husband. In the depiction of Tomazo, Middleton seems to be appealing to a stereotypical perception of Spanish culture in which the demand for revenge, identified with honour, is readily aroused. For Tomazo, as he accosts Vermandero, duty to family and honour are at stake: 'I claim a brother of you' (IV. ii. 17). Obliquely, he threatens retaliation against Vermandero's family if he finds no satisfaction: that is, if the murderer is not brought to account. It is, of course, heavily ironic that initially Tomazo perceives De Flores as a possible accomplice in his quest for retribution. That he so misconceives the situation also betrays his feelings of desperation at failing to solve what he thinks, but cannot be certain, is a crime. The effect of this futile search for the criminal is registered in Tomazo's soliloquy in the final act: since he is ignorant of the identity of his enemy, all friendship consequently has to be suspect. The next person he meets, he speculates, might be his brother's murderer; with the play's characteristic use of irony, De Flores is then seen to pass across the stage. Soon, however, Tomazo displays an instinctive unease in De Flores's presence; yet his suspicions about the latter's relationship with Beatrice do not extend to a conviction that De Flores might have murdered Alonzo.

In this state of blind ignorance where 'a brother may salute his brother's murderer' (V. ii. 47), Tomazo is ready to accept without question Vermandero's assertion that Franciscus and Antonio are guilty and he is quick to invoke the bloodthirsty language of the revenger. In thirsting for their blood he will, he declares, wind himself around them like lightning and melt their marrows. Vermandero has, of course, got the wrong men and the play does not require Tomazo to play out the role of revenger that he contemplates with such venom. In a series of revelations and peripeteia the climax of the play is reached and, in their last moments, the criminality of Beatrice and De Flores is exposed.

There is no categorical rejection of secular revenge in *The Changeling* as there is in *The Atheist's Tragedy*. Tomazo only comes to recognize the part of providence in achieving retribution when his own judgement is seen as erroneous. Even then, he is reluctant to relinquish his role and expresses a lingering wish to inflict further punishment on Beatrice Joanna and De Flores, as the pair, now desperate in their guilty passion, confess the murder (Fig. 9). After De Flores kills Beatrice and commits suicide, Tomazo expresses some satisfaction that justice and vengeance have finally been achieved:

> Sir, I am satisfied, my injuries
> Lie dead before me; I can extract no more,
> Unless my soul were loose, and could o'ertake
> Those black fugitives that are fled from thence,
> To take a second vengeance; but there are wraths
> Deeper than mine.

(V. iii. 190–5)

The 'wraths deeper than mine' – God's vengeance called upon but rarely represented in earlier plays – make *The Changeling*, if we accept the perspective of the survivors, a providential revenge play. Indeed, embedded in the play's imagery there is the sense of characters fatalistically playing out preordained parts. When Beatrice is desperately and self-deludedly trying to buy off De Flores for his murder of Alonzo, De Flores reiterates the view, in a fine conceit, that being the 'deed's creature' she cannot expect to escape the consequences. 'Can you weep fate from its determined purpose?' he questions, alluding to the inevitability of Beatrice repaying him for murder by becoming his lover. Yet ironically De Flores, so intent on possessing Beatrice, does not see beyond this desire. He does not follow his logical argument through to the conclusion that murder too must have a final reckoning.

The power and interest of *The Changeling* lie not in the psyche of the revenger or in any internalized dilemma about justice and revenge, but in the exploration of the murderers' partnership. In Beatrice's relationship with De Flores, love and revulsion are intertwined. She enticingly leans on him to murder an

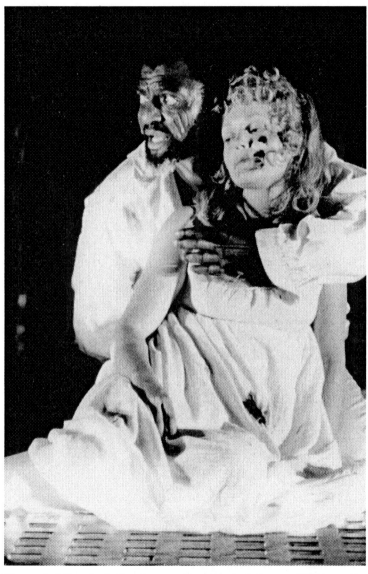

Figure 9. Miranda Richardson as Beatrice and George Harris as De Flores in the 1988 Royal National Theatre production of *The Changeling*, directed by Richard Eyre. With the permission of the photographer John Haynes.

undesired suitor and is incapable of recognizing that she is thus a murderer by proxy. De Flores presents her with the grisly token of his service to her – the severed figure of Alonzo de Piracquo on which is the ring she was obliged to give him. Reversing the symbolism of the bloody relics retained by other revengers, indicative of their inner trauma, she recoils with horror at the physical reminder of a deed she would like to forget – 'Bless me! What hast thou done?' – and is rebuked by De Flores – 'Is that more/ Than killing the whole man?'(III. iv. 29–30). Beatrice's moral naïvety gives way to increasingly wild attempts to escape discovery, while her revulsion from De Flores turns into total reliance. In the scene of Diaphanta's murder – on Beatrice's thwarted wedding night – she recognizes that her obligation is complete: 'I'm forced to love thee now/ 'Cause thou provid'st so carefully for my honour' (V. i. 47–8). In other revenge plays, 'honour' is appropriated or cynically manipulated to justify vengeance. Beatrice Joanna's concept of 'honour' is not invoked in the cause of revenge, although its dubious 'defence' does lead to murder. Middleton creates in Beatrice a woman who, in her persistent belief that involvement in murder is less abhorrent than loss of reputation, is guilty of self-delusion. Part of the play's fascination lies in her semi-psychotic state as she improvises morality and convinces herself that her actions are defensible. Her reiterated appeal to honour can be said, however, to be in part female indoctrination. Vermandero's response to the revelations of the final scene suggest that his daughter's sexual transgression is of greater moment than her involvement with Alonzo's murder. When De Flores confesses the love and pleasure he has had from Beatrice, Vermandero immediately threatens torture. That sexual submission and the loss of the appearance of virtue is more reprehensible than murder is apparently a moral code shared by father and daughter. Middleton would seem to be exposing the superficial nature of honour in this society: a judgement which is, by implication, extended to the portrayal of Tomazo and his ineffectual talk of revenge identified with the reparation of family honour.

The dramatic focus of *The Changeling* is on the criminal and the crime rather than on the revenger and retribution and this represents the compelling force of the play. As with *The Atheist's*

Tragedy, the evolution of events in *The Changeling* seems to be underpinned by a sense of nemesis, yet in *The Changeling* this is never to the detriment of psychological credibility. In *The Atheist's Tragedy* providence intervenes in a way that could be seen as crudely spectacular and as a provocation to laughter. There is nothing remotely conducive to laughter in the final moments of *The Changeling* when we witness the wretchedness of De Flores and Beatrice Joanna as they accept that their manoeuvrings to avoid retribution have been defeated.

4

Revenge out of Italy

In several Jacobean tragedies of revenge by John Webster, Thomas Middleton and John Ford, the setting of the play and the avenging figures are Italian. This could be seen as a projective device whereby the Italians, rather than the English, are seen as violent and cruel and, thus, foreignness becomes an audience's defence against a sense of its own destructiveness. Fantasies of revenge can be safely projected on an alien political and religious culture.[1] The Italian principalities, through popular association with crimes of blood, in their multifaceted aspects of murder, kin, passion and will, were the obvious choice of foreign location, and stories of crimes of passion, often of recent memory, were mediated through a range of sources including novella and travel writing. Many of these works expose the common prejudice that Italians were particularly prone to uncontrolled passions and collateral jealousies.[2] In Thomas Nashe's *The Unfortunate Traveller* (1594), when Jack Wilton, the eponymous traveller, is at the point of execution in Rome, he is saved by the intervention of a banished English earl. Displaying stereotypical notions of a vengeful Italian disposition, the earl warns Jack not to stay in Italy:

> If thou dost but lend half a look to a Roman's or Italian's wife, thy porridge shall be prepared for thee and cost thee nothing but thy life. Chance some of them break a bitter jest on thee and thou retortest it severely or seemest discontented, go to thy chamber and provide a great banquet, for thou shalt be sure to be visited with guests in a mask the next night when in kindness and courtship thy throat shall be cut and the doers return undiscovered. Nothing so long of memory as a dog; these Italians are old dogs and will carry an injury a whole age in memory. I have heard of a box on the ear that hath been revenged thirty year after.[3]

Jack Wilton disregards the earl's advice and, although he lives to tell the tale of his further adventures by prolonging his stay in Italy, he has several more scrapes with death. *The Unfortunate Traveller* exemplifies in parts of its narrative English folly and Italian vice, a paradigm that has been noted in a number of English Renaissance texts.[4] Such a view of the perfidious and vengeful Italian psyche was deeply ingrained and, since it bolstered a contrasting national self-image of moderation and temperance, it was very little questioned in works of the period.[5] In a chapter devoted to the subject of behaviour, in *The English Gentlewoman* (1631), Richard Braithwait opens a section on 'Passion' with the observation, 'What a furious and inconsiderate thing is woman, when passion distempers her' and warns that there are many examples of the fearful effects of emotions working themselves out as revenge, notably in Italy, 'which is a very theatre of tragic conclusions in this kind'.[6]

While the Italian location clearly gave English playwrights a degree of imaginative freedom in representing revenge, a practice ostensibly outlawed in England, it was not entirely a prejudiced, fictional construct. The political and social conditions of the Italian city states were such that revenge was more readily condoned and less circumscribed by law, than in England. The traveller Fynes Moryson, commenting on Italian justice, observed that malefactors could easily escape from the jurisdiction of one principality to another and, further, that the mutual jealousies of the princes ensured that offenders often escaped official prosecution.[7] The perceived difference between English criminal law, trial and punishment and Italian private vengeance as a mode of institutionalized retribution is exemplified in a case of 1612, mentioned in the Introduction to this book, concerning a Scottish noble, Lord Sanquire, brought to trial for the premeditated killing of a man who several years earlier had blinded him. The murder was a surrogate one, as Sanquire had, according to the trial verdict, 'hired two of his countrymen, men of low and mercenary spirits', to kill the fencing master John Turner. When Francis Bacon, Solicitor General, passed judgement, he made a point of appealing to the common assumption of the vengeful Italian spirit: 'I conceive you have sucked those affections of dwelling in malice rather out of Italy than out of any part of this island of

England and Scotland.'[8] Such a notion of a culturally permissible vengeance fed into theatre production for several decades, enabling constructions of revenge untenable in more local dramatic settings.

More relevant to the plays discussed in this chapter is the way revenge in Italy was seen to operate, notably to regulate personal – particularly female - conduct. Moryson comments:

> Adulteries (as all furies of jealousy, or signs of making love to wives, daughters and sisters) are commonly prosecuted by private revenge, and by murder, and the princes and judges, measuring their just revenge by their own passions proper to that nation, make no great enquiry after such murders besides that the revenging party is wise enough to do them secretly, or at least in disguised habit.[9]

Here we have the scenario and ingredients of the later Renaissance tragedy of revenge, where the call for violent and outlawed justice of earlier plays has been replaced by a drive to assuage slighted family honour and reputation. Clearly, clandestine passion, as a provocation to revenge, has considerable dramatic and theatrical capital, inviting ironic treatment of a morality skewed to equate murder and sexual transgression. The audience make a moral differentiation that the characters do not. The plays of Webster and Ford contain a number of scenes in which church and state are exposed as corrupting the rule of law and condoning murder. If Italy lent a new socio-political dimension to revenge tragedy, it also offered theatrical possibilties. In Moryson's stereotypical observation on the secrecy of revenge and the use of disguise in its pursuit, there is further dramatic potential for a genre which relies so heavily on acting and role playing as metaphors of deceit and dissembling. Such devices are fully exploited in all the plays discussed in this chapter.

THE WHITE DEVIL

John Webster seems to have begun his career working in collaboration with several of his contemporaries, including Thomas Middleton and Thomas Dekker, before developing the very distinctive dramatic and poetic style we see in *The White Devil* and *The Duchess of Malfi*. *The White Devil* was the first of two

Italian tragedies in which revenge, variously motivated amongst the characters, encloses the action. What lifts these tragedies above mere stories of grand passion set amidst family vendettas and courtly depravity is the arresting quality of the language. Webster's verse is visceral, densely imagistic in its exploitation of surprising simile and extended metaphor, and sententious and witty in its use of aphorism and proverb. Passages of agitated introspection are juxtaposed with startling generalizations about human and social conduct. As in other revenge plays, there are expressions of mordant black humour which are accompanied in Webster's drama by an underlying scepticism. Webster's characters are memorable for their restless subjectivity as they engage with objective stage action and, in the case of his female protagonists, exhibit an heroic defiance of male power and privilege.

The White Devil was first performed at the Red Bull theatre, a playhouse to the north of the city where the clientele was more citizen than gentry. Whatever the social constitution of the audience, however, it seems not to have appreciated *The White Devil*, since according to Webster's own testimony the play lacked 'a full and understanding auditory' when it was first performed.[10] The rather chaotic plotting and the introduction of event and character subsidiary to the main action may have brought about such a response. While individual scenes are memorably powerful, the sprawling action tends to hamper theatrical momentum and, in particular, the revenge dynamic of the play.

Revenge is ignited through crimes of passion. The Duke of Bracciano, out of his desire for Vittoria Corombona, plots the murder of his wife, Isabella, and Vittoria's husband Camillo, and this invites retaliation from powerful kin. Isabella's brother, Francisco de Medici, Duke of Florence, and Camillo's cousin Cardinal Monticelso plot revenge by proxy. Vittoria is the first to be targeted and, although there is no actual evidence against her, she is brought to trial; Bracciano is poisoned during his wedding celebrations and later Vittoria and her brother Flamineo are murdered. The narrative derives greater complexity and psychological depth from the characters of Flamineo and Count Lodovico, Francisco's instrument of revenge. Flamineo is, like Vindici in *The Revenger's Tragedy*, a malcontent, and, also like

Vindici, he becomes a pander to his own sister, although with the considerable difference that in *The White Devil* Flamineo and Vittoria are willingly the procurer and the procured. As Flamineo tells his honest brother Marcello, he is intent on self-advancement: 'I made a kind of path/ To her and mine own advancement' (III. i. 36–7). He turns viciously on his sister when, after the death of Bracciano, he sees all his ambitions thwarted. While the revenge motif assumes greater centrality after the climactic scene of Vittoria's arraignment, *The White Devil* can be seen also as representing a doomed pursuit of social mobility, as an ambitious middle-class family attempt to invade an aristocracy which wreaks revenge upon them for their social presumption.

The intrigue of *The White Devil* follows quite closely actual events in Padua in December 1585, when the Duke of Bracciano was mysteriously murdered. This followed the death of his first wife and his subsequent marriage to a woman from the Roman house of Accaramboni whose husband had recently been murdered.[11] In his dramatization, Webster develops the identity and motivations of the avengers so that the Machiavellian Francisco employs the notorious murderer Count Lodovico to revenge his sister's death. Lodovico has his own secret desire for vengeance: he confesses to Monticelso that he loved Bracciano's duchess or, rather, he 'pursued her with hot lust' and, knowing that she has been poisoned, he has sworn 't'avenge her murder' (IV. iii. 111–15). Through his complex intrigue and motivation, Webster exploits the circuitous and secretive pursuit of Italianate vengeance as it was described by Fynes Moryson.

At first, it is the Cardinal Monticelso who is intent on revenge, devising means of incriminating Bracciano in adultery. He admits that his conduct may be regarded as 'dishonourable', but speculates that in matters of family honour he would go to such extremes as 'stake a brother's life/ That being wrong'd durst not avenge himself' (II. i. 391–4). Monticelso's role is, however, superseded by that of Francisco, who displays all the cunning and duplicity of another princely avenger, Lorenzo in *The Spanish Tragedy*. Webster's construction of Francisco as the avenger is an interesting one. Unlike Lorenzo, Francisco does have a valid reason for pursuing vengeance: his sister has been poisoned so that her husband can marry another woman. Yet there is no expression of frustrated justice in Francisco's machinations. As Duke of Florence, Francisco assumes that he will act extra-legally to avenge a murder committed in another state. While his agent Lodovico is punished, there is no suggestion that the law will hold Francisco to account. Bracciano too remains immune from the law. Such immunity is blatantly an aristocratic privilege. Bracciano rashly promises Vittoria, as his mistress, that he will seat her 'above law and above scandal' (I. ii. 263). But, scandal is something that Vittoria, as a woman of a lower social order, cannot avoid, and, moreover, as her rigged trial demonstrates, the machinery of the law can be invoked against her. In the end, however, social rank is no protection: the rough justice of private vengeance operates equally against Vittoria, Flamineo and Bracciano.

As the object of the ruling class's vicious resentment, Vittoria is punished, not for a specific crime, but for daring to aspire beyond her class and for betraying her sensual nature. She may have wished for Camillo's murder, but it was not an act in which she was herself implicated. Vittoria is cornered and without defence at her trial: Webster allows her to compel admiration for her defiance and self-assertion as she denounces Monticelso for being accuser and judge and derides the proceedings for being conducted in Latin. Although he is at first present, Bracciano offers little support; she confronts her accusers alone and confounds their accusations of sexual licence and complicity in murder.

The law and its processes in *The White Devil* are seen to be a sham, not because, as in earlier revenge plays, the legal system is impervious to calls for justice, but because it is manipulated against Vittoria by Francisco and Monticelso and then, when it suits them, disregarded. In wreaking private revenge against Bracciano and Vittoria, Francisco embodies all the traits of the insidious avenger. When Monticelso reminds him that his sister has been poisoned, Francisco responds dispassionately: 'Far be it from my thoughts/ To seek revenge' (IV. i. 3–4). Once alone, Francisco reveals that he has no intention of revealing his plans to Monticelso, a would-be ally:

> Monticelso,
> I will not trust thee, but in all my plots
> I'll rest as jealous as a town besieg'd.
> Thou canst not reach what I intend to act;

> Your flax soon kindles, soon is out again,
> But gold slow heats, and long will hot remain.
>
> (IV. i. 37–42)

All the cunning of the stage Machiavel is revealed in the images of Francisco's lines. To stimulate his fashioning of revenge, curiously, he demands to see his sister's face and conjures up her ghost, an apparition that has such little stage presence that Francisco remains unmoved by its appearance: 'what have I to do/ With tombs, or death beds, funerals, or tears/ That have to meditate upon revenge' (IV. i. 113–15). A token of revenge tragedy is evoked and then disregarded as Francisco distances himself from the avenger's conventional responses. He declares that he scorns 'to wear a sword and prate of wrong' and disdains active engagement even as he plots coolly to deploy killers to avenge the family honour.

When he employs Lodovico as his agent, Francisco cynically appropriates the ritual and language of revenge as duty: 'You have ta'en the sacrament to prosecute/ The intended murder' (IV. iii. 72–3). Lodovico supplies the bloodthirsty passion associated with earlier stage avengers and absent in the Machiavellian intrigue of his employee. After the murder of Vittoria and Flamineo, it is Lodovico who exhibits all the exultation of the avenger:

> I do glory yet,
> That I can call this act mine own: – for my part,
> The rack, the gallows, and the torturing wheel
> Shall be but sound sleeps to me, – here's my rest –
> I limb'd this night-piece and it was my best.
>
> (V. vi. 293–7)

The rhetoric here has resonances of that of earlier avengers in that 'rest' can only come with the satisfaction of revenge, but the context is quite different. As the last line illustrates, Lodovico's act of vengeance, as he sees it, represents his finest hour. The play opens with his angry reaction to his banishment from Rome and his intense resentment against Fortune for what he sees as his social subjugation. He is judged, as one of his followers tells him, 'an idle meteor' by the nobility. Lodovico's revenge on Bracciano and the Corombona family has no real motivation of justice. He pays lip service to the notion of righting a wrong when he refers to his love for Isabella, but this feeling is never reiterated. Instead, in satisfying self-elevation and in serving as some kind of reparation for what he sees as lack of social and material advantage, it is an imaginary form of compensation.

Clearly, the pursuit of an outlawed justice is not, as in earlier revenge plays, at stake in *The White Devil*. In its theatrical aesthetics, specifically its feel for the visually spectacular, the play does, however, have links with earlier tragedies. Webster's often garish verbal imagery is matched by an equivalent use of visual image. The deaths of Camillo and Isabella, which Bracciano has orchestrated, are shown to him in dumb show. Isabella dies by kissing the lips of Bracciano's portrait and this death by poison is then repeated in Bracciano's own murder as he dons a helmet poisoned by Lodovico. Later Bracciano's ghost appears to Flamineo to sprinkle earth upon him and reveal a skull, which we recognize as a portent of Flamineo's death. The ghost, like the earlier apparition of Isabella, is little more than a stage device, since it neither bears a message nor seeks to extract any promise from the beholder. In the agnostic and morally confusing world Webster projects, where revenge is purely a secular affair, ghosts carry little supernatural symbolism and are merely part of Webster's ornamentation.

In the final act of *The White Devil*, Webster translates Fynes Moryson's account of the disguise and secrecy that shrouds Italian revenge into brilliant theatrical images. Having played no direct part in the killing, Francisco, dressed as a Moor, silently witnesses the prolonged and agonizing death of Bracciano while the conspirators Lodovico and Gasparo, disguised as Capuchin monks, profess to bring him the last rites and then attend him *'with a crucifix and hallowed candle'* (Fig. 10). The death scene of Vittoria and Flamineo is remarkable for its reversals. Flamineo first tries to trick Vittoria into suicide by demanding that she shoot him before turning her weapon on herself. Thinking she has done the deed, Vittoria discloses that she has no intention of killing herself, whereupon Flamineo rises to reveal that the pistols were not loaded. When Vittoria and Flamineo have eluded each other's murderous intentions, the revengers enter – still disguised as Capuchins – to complete their task. The death scene again demonstrates Webster's theatrical technique as

Figure 10. Dennis Quilley as Bracciano in the 1991 Royal National Theatre production of *The White Devil*. With the permission of the photographer Ivan Kyncl.

Flamineo and Vittoria meet their pitiless ends without a jot of self-pity. 'Churchmen turned revellers' is how Flamineo sardonically greets the avengers. The appropriation of religious iconography – as in *The Duchess of Malfi* when Julia kisses a poisoned Bible – in the service of revenge is all part of the persistent moral turbulence of Webster's revenge plays.

The intervention of Giovanni, Bracciano's young son, at the end of the play, issuing a warning to 'guilty men', is perfunctory. There is no suggestion that Francisco will be or could be called to account and no sense of moral or political cleansing. The deaths of Vittoria and Flamineo are part of the internal logic of the play in which the ruling class are viciously resentful of a lower-middle-class family that attempts to enter their order.

THE DUCHESS OF MALFI

Webster's second major tragedy, *The Duchess of Malfi*, is set in the same Renaissance world as *The White Devil*, that of rival Italian city states dominated by corrupt churchmen and tyrannical princes. In the latter play, though, revenge is activated by one duke against another and directed at a socially aspirant family, whereas in *The Duchess of Malfi* revenge is mobilized from within the same family. The widowed Duchess of Malfi refuses to be controlled by her corrupt brothers, who have forbidden her to remarry, and when she secretly does so, and to a man of inferior rank, she provokes their sadistic retaliation. The infiltration of the aristocracy from below, which is a catalyst in both *The White Devil* and *The Duchess of Malfi*, is far less deliberate in the marriage of the Duchess to her steward, whose role in the relationship is essentially passive, wooed as he is by the Duchess, and clandestine.

Stemming from Senecan tragedy, one of the motifs of early Renaissance revenge tragedies is that the act of retribution exceeds in ferocity the original crime. There is a perversion of this notion of a wrong outweighed by reprisal in Webster's play. In marrying her steward, Antonio, the Duchess has behaved in an unorthodox way by challenging the dominant view that a woman should marry for the advantage of the family, but she has not committed in any sense a crime.[12] The Duchess may be driven by passion and she may be refusing to fulfil the duties of her class, but the play offers no condemnation of her desires and, indeed, Webster consistently presents her as noble and courageous. In attempting to deter her from any remarriage, Ferdinand, Prince of Calabria, and the Cardinal harangue their sister menacingly and Ferdinand threatens her with his dagger. In response, the Duchess's soliloquy is defiant and resolute:

> If all my royal kindred
> Lay in my way unto this marriage,
> I'd make them my low footsteps: and even now,
> Even in this hate, as men in some great battles,
> By apprehending danger, have achiev'd
> Almost impossible actions – I have heard soldiers say so –
> So I, through frights, and threatenings, will assay
> This dangerous venture: let old wives report
> I wink'd and chose a husband.

> (I. i. 341–9)

There is a recklessness in the Duchess's assertions and actions – as Cariola, her waiting woman, later comments – but she also compels admiration for her determination and autonomy faced with her brothers' oppression. In the above soliloquy she appropriates masculine, martial imagery – she will overcome the odds in battle through her bold actions – in the domestic context of choosing her own husband. The consequences of such self-direction are horrendous as Ferdinand moves to avenge himself upon his twin sister, her husband and her children.

The response of Ferdinand to the news reported to him by the intelligencer Bosola that his sister has conducted a secret relationship and has had a child, is excessive, hinting at unacknowledged desires. He demands the most sadistic of punishments. Yoking the verbal and visual, he displays to his brother the handkerchief that he claims he will bequeath to their sister's 'bastard'. In answer to the Cardinal's enquiry of his reason for the bequest, he projects imaginary vengeance: 'Why, to make soft lint for his mother's wounds,/ When I have hew'd her to pieces' (II. v. 30–31). Once she is in his power, imprisoned on his order, Ferdinand is in a position to practise all his sadistic imaginings and he is driven by a desire to inflict physical pain and mental torture on his sister that have little relation to her transgression. He contrives to break the Duchess's spirit by having her set upon by madmen and she is further tormented by the shape-changing Bosola, who acts under Ferdinand's instructions to bring his sister to a state of despair before her murder.

One of the most powerful episodes of Jacobean theatre is the harrowing sequence leading to the death of the Duchess; a protracted enactment of perverted revenge that is countered majestically by the Duchess. The scene contains gradations of emotion that place considerable demands on the actress. Following her loud agony of grief on being shown the dead bodies, as she thinks, of her family, the Duchess becomes more contained, enduring the torment of the mad folk at her door with remarkable fortitude. When Cariola alludes to Ferdinand's tyranny, the Duchess replies calmly, if paradoxically: 'Indeed, I thank him, nothing but noise and folly/ Can keep me in my right wits, whereas reason/ And silence make me stark mad' (IV. ii. 5–7). By the time the Duchess faces death, she seems already beyond any physical torment her torturers can inflict. She remains unmoved by the sinister presence of Bosola, who in various guises lurks in the chamber, impressing upon her the fearsomeness of death:

> BOSOLA. Yet, methinks,
> The manner of your death should much afflict you,
> This cord should terrify you?
> DUCHESS.   Not a whit:
> What would it pleasure me to have my throat cut
> With diamonds? Or to be smothered
> With cassia? Or to be shot to death with pearls ...
>   Tell my brothers
> That I perceive death, now I am well awake,
> Best gift is they can give, or I can take.
>
>   (IV. ii. 213–25)

The Duchess's resilience under mental torment and the manner in which she faces her death ensure that her moral victory over her brothers is an absolute one. In no other play is revenge seen as such a moral perversion against such an innocent victim.

When he sees the corpse of his sister, Ferdinand expresses his emotion in the staccato rhythm of the line 'Cover her face; mine eyes dazzle; she died young': a line that Bosola caps with the twisted yet compassionate words 'I think not so: her infelicity/ Seem'd to have years too many.' Bosola and Ferdinand have the same relationship of instrument and revenger as Lodovico and Francisco in *The White Devil*. All are equally implicated in murder, but Ferdinand's ducal status, like that of Francisco, allows him to control, dominate and, finally, disown his instrument of revenge. He banishes Bosola: 'Get thee into some unknown part o'th'world/ That I may never see thee' (IV. ii. 326–7). Bosola sets out for Milan to find fresh employment, harbouring thoughts of revenge against his superiors for his banishment now that he is perceived to have outlived his usefulness. In contrast, following the death of his sister, Ferdinand's mental disintegration is complete; his psychotic state is revealed in the peculiar disease of lycanthropy that afflicts him, whereby he thinks himself a ravening wolf.

In defying her brothers the Duchess clearly arouses Ferdinand's sadistic impulses. Before her death, Ferdinand comments obliquely and sententiously on his state of mind: 'Intemperate agues make physicians cruel' (IV. i. 142). But the exact motives for his inordinate reaction remain dark and understated. After his sister's murder, Ferdinand attempts to rationalize his motivation:

> What were the meanness of her match to me?
> Only I must confess, I had a hope,
> Had she continu'd widow, to have gain'd
> An infinite mass of treasure by her death:
> And that was the main cause: . . . her marriage! –
> That drew a stream of gall, quite through my heart.
>
> (IV. ii. 282–7)

This is the only allusion in the play to Ferdinand's mercenary ambitions and as an exploration of conscious action it is unconvincing. The literal text provides no ready explanation for Ferdinand's obsessive vendetta against the Duchess and this is part of the psychological fascination of the drama.[13] Webster's plays hint at the unconscious: the pressures towards action within the personality that are subjectively unrecognized for what they are. As we see from his reaction to the idea of her marriage and procreation, Ferdinand is obsessed with his sister's sexuality. Once he has heard that his sister has had a child, his rage is conveyed in images of sex and violence, as he imagines his sister with 'some strong thigh'd bargeman . . . or else some lovely squire/ That carries coals up to her privy lodgings' (II. v. 42–5). In psychoanalytical terms, we can see how the peculiarities of Ferdinand's behaviour fit aspects of Freud's analysis of melancholia in his classic thesis 'Melancholia and Mourning'. Love for an object which cannot be given up, even though it is renounced, can result in taking revenge against the object and deriving sadistic satisfaction from its suffering.[14] There is certainly a suggestion that Ferdinand harbours incestuous feelings towards his sister and that these submerged impulses fuel his desire to inflict such hideous torment on her and to take pleasure in observing that torment.

After the Duchess's death and Ferdinand's descent into madness, the focus of the play shifts to Bosola and consequently a second revenge plot is activated. As an intelligencer and a sardonic, cynical malcontent, Bosola is Webster's creation. His role, however, extends beyond that of the disaffected outsider in the pay of social superiors, and in the final act the perverted logic of his actions becomes clear. He was at first loyal to the Cardinal, then to Ferdinand, and then, after the Duchess's death, his own sense of outrage leads him to seek some kind of reparation. Like Flamineo in *The White Devil*, he is a study of misplaced intelligence but, unlike Flamineo, it could also be said that he is not as wholly corrupted. Bosola betrays those who trust him, but he is also betrayed. He advises the Duchess to take flight once her marriage has been discovered – betrayed by him to Ferdinand – and she more or less walks into an ambush. In his turn, Bosola is betrayed by Ferdinand and it is this and the haunting effect of the Duchess's death which produce the hope of saving Antonio from the revenge of the Cardinal and a belated desire for expiation:

> Well, good Antonio,
> I'll seek thee out, and all my care shall be
> To put thee into safety from the reach
> Of these most cruel biters, that have got
> Some of thy blood already. It may be
> I'll join with thee, in a most just revenge.
> The weakest arm is strong enough, that strikes
> With the sword of justice: – still methinks the duchess
> Haunts me.

(V. ii. 338–46)

Bosola evokes the rhetoric of earlier revenge plays in equating revenge with the 'sword of justice'. The linear plot of retribution that is anticipated in Bosola's perverse strategy of revenging the murder that he has committed is not, though, fulfilled according to design. The final scenes show spiralling destruction as events happen by accident and with moral arbitrariness. Bosola stabs Antonio, believing him to be the Cardinal; Ferdinand kills the Cardinal and wounds Bosola, whose last act is to kill Ferdinand. The scheme to revenge the Duchess's death thus unwittingly leads to that of her husband. Bosola is at a loss when asked to account for Antonio's death: 'In a mist: I know not how – /Such a mistake as I have often seen/ In a play' (V. v. 94–6). Here the commonplace stage metaphor is employed back on itself to capture an unpredictability alien to the inner logic of the revenge play. There is no triumphant revenger or revengers in *The Duchess of Malfi*; there is only Bosola's half-awakened conscience for the death of the Duchess, embedded in his dying thought that it is no harm to die 'in so good a quarrel'.

WOMEN BEWARE WOMEN

In *Women Beware Women* Thomas Middleton dramatized Italian material contemporaneous with that depicted in Webster's *The White Devil*. Middleton's Duke of Florence is the Francisco of Webster's play. Although the murder of the Duke's sister Isabella by her husband Paolo Giordano Orsini represented in *The White Devil* and the Duke's liaison with Bianca Cappello dramatized in *Women Beware Women* were concurrent events, there is no overlap of the respective dramatic narratives and the Medici duke is rather differently represented in the two plays. Francisco is a scheming Machiavellian avenger, while the middle-aged Duke of *Women Beware Women* is a rapt sensualist who out of self-interest seizes the opportunity casually to prompt ideas of revenge in another.[15] It is only in the final act of Middleton's tragedy that revenge, a recurring motif in Webster's re-creation of the feuding aristocracy, dominates the action so that virtually none of the original cast survives.

Despite the fact that they exploit similar source material, Webster and Middleton produce quite different tragic and revenge drama from it. In the equation of crime and retribution and in the image of self-destructiveness that is so central to *Women Beware Women*, there is an inexorable moral argument which is absent in the more provisional, ambivalent moral structures of *The White Devil*. We can see this difference of perspective in the representation of the female protagonists. Vittoria in *The White Devil* and Bianca in *Women Beware Women* are of similar social status and it could be said that they both use their sexuality – as their only asset in the class and patriarchal system – for social advancement. There is a difference, though, in that, confronted by her male predators, Vittoria is contained and assertive, while Bianca is more acted upon. Following her rape by the Duke, Bianca passively accepts and adjusts to her role as his mistress for its material advantage. As her epithets 'white devil' and 'devil in crystal', convey, the nature of Vittoria's involvement in the deaths of Camillo and Isabella cannot be ascertained; she responds scornfully to her detractors and at her trial refuses to behave as she is expected to. Bianca is less complex, represented as corrupted by power and privilege as she plots to be avenged on her detractor, the Cardinal. The nexus of class and money, in contradistinction to class and power, figures more prominently in Middleton's socially realistic milieu than in the court locations of Webster. The scene in *Women Beware Women* in which Bianca and Leantio, now the lover of the wealthy widow Livia, meet and each admire the fashionable, expensive clothes of the other, as signs of their social advancement (iv.i), is indicative of Middleton's preoccupation with commodified relationships.

In *Women Beware Women* Middleton was attracted to the story of Bianca Cappello, who in 1563, at the age of 16, had eloped from Venice to Florence with Pietro Bonaventuri (the Leantio of Middleton's play).[16] With their honour at stake, the Cappello family were eager for revenge and the two lovers were forced to live barricaded in their lodgings before seeking the protection and intercessions of Francesco de Medici. Middleton ignores this aspect of the story to focus on the rape of Bianca by the Duke and her ready accommodation to her role as the Duke's lover. In actuality, Bianca lived as the Duke's mistress for several years while he was married to Joanna of Austria and during this time Pietro's career and court position were advanced. In 1572

Pietro, like Leantio, was murdered by a relative of one of his lovers, who was herself murdered the following day. Here, historical event is mirrored in *Women Beware Women* as the lower-class Leantio is murdered by Hippolito, the brother of Livia, who is incensed by what he sees as an insult to family honour. This first act of revenge is represented characteristically by Middleton as coloured by moral hypocrisy rather than driven by any real desire to redeem honour. The Duke, who wants Leantio removed, incites Hippolito to revenge and Hippolito is a ready instrument. As a motive for revenge, Middleton exposes the opportunist manipulation of honour. In relation to Livia's association with Leantio, Hippolito is in no position to preach of honour and morality since he is himself conducting an incestuous relationship with his niece. In his soliloquy before he kills Leantio, Hippolito acknowledges that he too is 'monstrously guilty', but that there is a 'blind time' in which Leantio could have pursued his desire; in effect, if Leantio had employed more subterfuge he would have been less guilty (IV. ii. 1–10). Here there is a typical conflation of public appearance, which in essence is what has drawn Hippolito to vengeance, and a skewed sense of morality.

As is the common practice in Renaissance plays, Middleton telescopes historical events and dispenses with detail that is irrelevant to dramatic patterning and theatrical effect. In reality, following the death of the Grand Duchess – ignored in the play – the duke married Bianca Cappello and they lived together for nine years before their deaths, which came within one day of each other in October 1587. The Duke's brother was present at the villa where the deaths occurred and contemporaries drew conclusions from his presence about the nature of his involvement. In *Women Beware Women* the revenge plot is heightened by having the Duke and Bianca die during the wedding celebrations (as in the murder of Bracciano in *The White Devil*) and by multiple conspiracies which go ironically awry. Middleton incorporates into the revenge designs of Bianca against the Cardinal those of Livia against Hippolito and Isabella against Livia.

Exploiting the device of vengeance under guise of entertainment, also represented in *The Spanish Tragedy* and *The Revenger's Tragedy*, Middleton depicts mass murder during the wedding masque of the Duke and Bianca, involving all the characters. As Guardiano tells Livia, performance offers a certain impunity: mischiefs will be thought/ Things merely accidental – all's by chance,/ Not got of their own natures (IV. ii. 164–6). The remark is ironically prescient. Events do indeed turn out to be dictated by accident and chance, as the Duke drinks from the poisoned cup intended for his brother and Guardiano falls through the trap door instead of Hippolito. In these domino-like final scenes of the play, as one murder is seen to match another, all the characters lose themselves in vengeful intentions. In a perverse way, despite the obvious theatricality in the manner of the murders, revenge becomes psychologically accurate, effectively endemic to the natures of characters driven by thwarted desire. Bent on nothing but self-fulfilment, the egotistical response is to destroy any seeming agent of obstruction, as is the case with Bianca and Livia.

There is no sustained vendetta of revenge dictating the plot in *Women Beware Women* as there is in the plays of Webster. The perversion of human relationships we see throughout the play is configured in the disparate revenges of the masque as niece kills aunt, sister kills brother and wife, accidentally, kills husband. The dying Hippolito recognizes all the destructive impulses at work: 'Vengeance met vengeance/ Like a set match, as if the plagues of sin/ Had been agreed to meet here altogether.' (V. ii. 157–9) Such words, as has been noted, are spoken not by a character with credible psychology, but by a performer in the masque of retribution.[17] Hippolito articulates what the play as a whole seems to endorse – a sense of moral retribution in the enactment of revenge which is not attributable to any single moral agency.

'TIS PITY SHE'S A WHORE

The plays of John Ford, mostly composed during the reign of Charles I, have been seen as recuperating and reworking themes and preoccupations of earlier Elizabethan and Jacobean drama.[18] Although poetically less intricate, there are certainly structural similarities and recall of motif between *Romeo and Juliet* and *'Tis Pity She's a Whore*. Likeness, however, subsists in formal aspects rather than in the essence of the plays. In both plays the lovers are doomed because their love is forbidden and in each play a friar and a female servant know about the clandestine relationship. Giovanni is in part a Romeo consumed by passion, but he also has affinities with overreaching figures represented in the plays of Christopher Marlowe. Giovanni, a man of intellect, defies providential belief; but, in rejecting orthodox teaching on incest which impedes his love for his sister, Giovanni's defiance is both religiously and socially transgressive. Although incest was not a new theme to tragedy – it was represented by Middleton in *Women Beware Women* – it had not previously been confronted so directly or with such intensity. In depicting the two lovers Ford achieves a fine balance between sympathy for genuine passion and a recognition of its essentially subversive character.

The play's location in the Italian city of Parma affiliates *'Tis Pity She's a Whore* not only with the tragedy of doomed love in *Romeo and Juliet* (set in Verona), but also with the revenge tragedies of Middleton and Webster. Ford similarly exploits the literary and cultural stereotype of Italians as settling their rivalries and sexual jealousies through private vengeance, and in so doing he surpasses earlier Italianate tragedies in the spectacular nature of the revenge taken. In the final act Soranzo, Annabella's husband, upon learning of his wife's pregnancy and the relationship with her brother, devises his revenge aided by his Spanish servant Vasques and by banditti, murderers outlawed from one state to another. The assassins are promised pardon for previous murders if they commit this one and here, as in Ford's treatment of the Cardinal and other corrupt churchmen, the play affords a scenario of blatant double standards. The scene in which Soranzo, Vasques and the anonymous banditti seal their plot imitates the ritual of revenge, but, as is clear from the emphasis on financial payment, it is a revenge devoid of any sense of honour or of justice:

> SORANZO You will not fail, or shrink in the attempt?
> VASQUES I will undertake for their parts: be sure, my masters, to be bloody enough, and as unmerciful as if you were preying upon a rich booty on the very mountains of Liguria. For your pardons, trust to my lord; but for reward you shall trust none but your own pockets.
> BANDITTI (*omnes*) We'll make a murder.

SORANZO Here's gold, here's more; want nothing, what you do
Is noble, and an act of brave revenge:
I'll make ye rich, banditti, and all free.
BANDITTI (*Omnes*) Liberty! Liberty! . . .
VASQUES In, then; your ends are profit and preferment – away!

(V. iv. 1–18)

The banditti, in effect, serve as mercenaries to Soranzo as he
plots the murders of Giovanni and Annabella at his birthday
feast. Ford builds up audience anticipation of the murderous
dénouement under the guise of feasting and entertainment,
such as we have seen in *The Spanish Tragedy*, *Antonio's Revenge*,
The Revenger's Tragedy and *Women Beware Women*. We are led to
expect the public exposure and murder of Giovanni and
Annabella in the presence of a triumphant Soranzo.

Such expectations are startlingly reworked as Giovanni,
warned by Annabella that the banquet is 'an harbinger of
death', pre-empts Soranzo in revenge, as he had earlier pre-
empted him in marriage. In the scene of the feast, at the line
when Soranzo enquires of his whereabouts, Giovanni enters on
cue with a heart impaled on his dagger, proclaiming his pride
'in the spoil/ Of love and vengeance'. Soranzo's immediate
response – 'Shall I be forestalled?' – captures his angry
resentment as he realizes that he has been outwitted by
Giovanni. Giovanni's consciousness of such rivalry is fully
exposed in his soliloquy following the murder of Annabella,
when he boasts that he has prevented Soranzo's 'reaching plots'
by performing the murder himself, thus becoming 'a most
glorious executioner'. The juxtaposition of 'glorious' and
'executioner', as in the later 'love' and 'vengeance', indicates
how distorted Giovanni's thinking has become. In their ego-
driven logic both Giovanni and Soranzo judge Annabella
'faithless' and this perverse thinking dictates their revenge.
Giovanni, however, in keeping with his volatile character,
expresses conflicting judgements of Annabella. In their last
encounter, his accusation of faithlessness is followed by his
assertion of Annabella's purity. Clearly intoxicated with the act
he is about to perform, he commends his lover/sister to heaven:
'Since we must part,/ Go thou white in thy soul, to fill a throne/
Of innocence and sanctity in Heaven' (V. v. 63–5). These are
curious words from a man who elsewhere in the play seems to

111

have rejected conventional notions of heaven and hell and they suggest that Ford is sacrificing psychological credibility for high emotion. The exhilaration of revenge that Giovanni feels is prolonged as he reveals to the appalled guests that the heart on his dagger – a shocking re-presentation of the Renaissance image of Cupid's shaft piercing the lover's heart – is that of his sister. His revenge is completed in the murder of Soranzo. There is a crazy hubris in his claim, spoken as he stabs Soranzo, that he will exchange Annabella's heart for Soranzo's living heart: 'Thus I exchange it royally for thine,/ And thus, and thus; now brave revenge is mine' (V. vi. 73–4).

The semiotics of revenge are here powerfully indicative of Giovanni's distraction. His possessive passion leads him to take Annabella's heart when he can no longer possess the body, and then return the organ, the most visceral relic that any revenger has carried, but now shorn of any mystical significance, to his rival in exchange for Soranzo's heart and vengeance. Giovanni's state of ecstasy following the murder of Annabella exaggerates the stance of earlier exultant, life-defying avengers. It is his moment of self-recompense, as he seems to have fulfilled his own absolute prophecy to Annabella: 'Love me, or kill me, sister.' The very extremity of his actions is consonant with the acts of earlier stage avengers, but in the case of Giovanni, there is no commensurate feeling of outraged injustice, no original crime that his revenge must outweigh. The logic of Giovanni's revenge is so twisted that its symbolism is elusive. We could see a sublimity in Giovanni's madness and certainly Ford has produced sensational theatre in the visual image of the heart on the dagger and in the bravura of the poetry as Giovanni alludes to the glory of his deed that 'darkened the mid-day sun, made noon at night'. Yet, equally, we could say there is as much resonance and more meaning in the pathos of Annabella's dying words, 'Brother, unkind, unkind', than there is in Giovanni's triumphant but disjunctive revenge rhetoric.

Ford's representation of the love of Giovanni and Annabella transmutes into revenge tragedy only in the final scenes of 'Tis Pity She's a Whore. From the beginning, though, as in other Italianate tragedies, recourse to revenge to settle wrong or a slight to honour is seen as endemic to life in Parma. In the second scene of the play Vasques, a Spaniard, and Grimaldi, a

Roman, engage in a fight ignited by rivalry over Annabella. Vasques, whose violent, revengeful nature is exposed as the drama evolves, is defending, as he does again later in the play, the claim of his master to Annabella and he is unperturbed by Grimaldi's threat of revenge. In a colloquial reformulation of the cognates of revenge, appetite and satiation, Vasques scornfully tells Grimaldi that he does not fear his 'honest innocence', as he knows Grimaldi's appetite will be satisfied enough on broth or soft food. Indeed, Grimaldi's ineffectuality as a revenger is borne out by subsequent developments as he is manipulated by Richardetto to revenge himself against Soranzo. Richardetto has his own motives for vengeance since his wife Hippolita has betrayed him with Soranzo. Hence there is another revenge plot threading its way through the drama, but one which fizzles out when Grimaldi kills the wrong man and – in a display of corrupt justice – is pardoned by the Cardinal, ironically the same man who passes judgement on Annabella as 'a whore'.

In the sub-revenge plot involving Richardetto, Hippolita and Soranzo, there is a diversity of interest as Richardetto and Hippolita plot independently against Soranzo. Again, the familiar trope of revenge enacted during entertainment is evoked as Hippolita plots to poison Soranzo during his wedding banquet. She appears disguised as a masque performer, and then unmasks in order to expose Soranzo's past and the false promises he has made to her. Vasques is entrusted with the deed, but being loyal to his master, he gives Hippolita the poisoned cup of wine instead of Soranzo and her revenge is aborted, to cries of justice from those present. It is all the more surprising, then, that when Soranzo and Vasques plot revenge against Giovanni and Annabella, they include 'Hippolita's blood' (V. iv. 23) in their cause, as if they had had no involvement in her murder. Here, as elsewhere in the play, pretexts are randomly invoked to justify bloody action in a way that exhibits the double standards prevalent in Parmese society.

'Now you begin to turn Italian', comments Vasques as Soranzo resolves to be revenged on Giovanni. In the event it is Vasques who kills Giovanni, and his exultation at the deed is expressed in terms of national identity: "Tis well: this conquest is mine, and I rejoice that a Spaniard outwent an Italian in revenge.' Vasques's vengeance, though, hardly competes in theatrical terms with that of Giovanni's, whose act surpasses that of any other stage Italian. *'Tis Pity She's a Whore* exceeds in stage effect and intemperate emotion any other English Renaissance tragedy that makes revenge Italian-style its focus. An English audience, secure in the knowledge of its cultural difference, might feel a voyeuristic pleasure in the acting out of such private passions in the public playhouse.

5

The Woman's Part

The revenge protagonists and antagonists of English Renaissance drama are almost exclusively male. Restitution of honour
was not a female vocation and to take revenge against a woman
was recognized, in a circular judgement, as deplorably 'womanish', transgressing codes of masculinity.[1] A woman's reputation
– her honour – was almost exclusively bound up with chastity;
this was regarded as the property of the male – father, brother,
husband, lover – and, if honour was damaged, this was an insult
to male kin and avenged in the name of father or husband.
Where there were male defenders of the family, the woman's
role in the reparation of wrong or the recovery of honour, was to
remain essentially passive. When women such as Antonio's wife
in *The Revenger's Tragedy* and Lavinia in *Titus Andronicus* are
raped, they kill themselves or are killed by next of kin, and this
is seen, for the violated female, as the proper course of action,
the only way to redeem male honour.[2]

In representations of sexual coercion, violence and retaliation,
the role of the woman in revenge tragedy is, however, more
than that of victim. In Thomas Heywood's *The Rape of Lucrece*
(1608), Lucrece, following the classical sources of the play,
commits suicide after her violation by Sextus Tarquin, declaring
that she prides 'her life less than her honoured fame'. But before
she dies, she is instrumental in inciting Junius Brutus, her father
and her husband to rise against and depose Tarquin. Without
her incitement, there would be no rebellion and no challenge to
tyranny. The situation is turned to male advantage as Brutus
displays Lucrece's body in the market place to kindle 'a most just
revenge'. In *Titus Andronicus*, the mutilated Lavinia has no
tongue to urge her cause, but, as she holds the bowl between her

stumps to catch the blood as the throats of her ravishers are slit, she is not simply a passive spectator of Titus's revenge.

Women may incite revenge, act as accomplices or be the initial cause of vendetta, but they rarely wield the knife. The combination of physical weakness and conventional notions of female passivity disempowered the would-be female avenger.[3] In female conduct books such as *The English Gentlewoman*, the unruly emotions of vengeance were seen as anathema to the female psyche, the author cautioning against destructive passion and urging women to suffer their wrongs with patience.[4] Few female characters in revenge plays transgress these boundaries, yet, within the confines, they are seen as urging and goading their tardy male kin into action. The very diversity of such female roles, circumventing tacit social prescriptions, defies any neat categorization, as playwrights re-presented the dynamic of revenge in different relationships and contexts.

Whatever the practice, the impulse to revenge has been identified as a feminine one.[5] In classical mythology, the Furies or Erinyes were the goddesses of vendettas and an appeal to them was the instigation of revenge. The Furies were also seen as personalized curses, since the curse was interpreted not as words alone, but as a potent force in stirring up mysterious powers to action. In the opening act of *Medea*, Seneca depicts Medea resolving to revenge herself against Jason and addressing the Furies as 'powers of feuding vengeance'. The concept of 'turning Fury', said of a woman by a man, denigrates the female by signifying frenzied, uncontrolled emotion, but it also underlies male anxiety at the power the female curse might unleash. The curse represents a descriptive, imaginative death and as such was appropriated as a female weapon. In *Richard III*, Queen Elizabeth and Queen Margaret, while they remain political enemies, lament jointly their loss of kin and their helplessness against male power and violence. Yet, they recognize that they still have imprecatory power. Elizabeth appeals to Margaret, 'O thou, well skilled in curses, stay a while,/ And teach me how to curse mine enemies' (IV. iv.110–11). Learning to curse, Margaret replies, involves intensifying feelings of love for that which is lost and of hate towards the murderer: a condition which raises parallels with the male avenger's state of mind. Margaret has to

concede that cursing may activate nothing; but it does nonetheless, like revenge, 'ease the heart'.

Vengeance itself, 'Vindicta', is personified and apostrophized
as feminine. But can we attach notions of gender to what, as has
been argued in this book, is a deeply rooted instinct, cross-
cultural and pan-historical? Arguably, female desire for vengeance is more strongly felt and articulated because it is mostly a
frustrated desire, only to be satisfied through a curse or male
agency. Deprived of a direct outlet of action, the woman
compensates by an imaginary vengeance. There are problems
with defining revenge in terms of gender derived from classical
myth: the identity of the Furies was not stable. In the final play
of Aeschylus's *Oresteia, The Eumenides*, the Furies begin as
vengeful dog-like creatures, insisting that they track down
'mortals overcome/ insane to murder kin'; at the end of the play
they have been transformed – and renamed the Eumenides –
into trusting human women.[6] Revenge may have been
personified as feminine, but, then, in Renaissance literature
many abstractions and personifications, including Fortune,
Necessity and Nature, are presented as female and endowed
with supposedly female characteristics. Gender associations
were flexible, used as they suited the dramatic purpose: Fortune,
for example, could be 'a right whore' (*The White Devil*) or
'bountiful' and a 'dear Lady' (*The Tempest*). As we have seen,
vengeance carried a similar range of signification, from
passionate calls for justice to the ego tyranny of Lorenzo and
Balthazar in *The Spanish Tragedy*.

In classical mythology, stories of female avengers ran to
excess and confusion. Medea in Seneca's play is part human,
part sorceress and part goddess as, having murdered her
children, she escapes through heaven in a serpent-drawn
chariot. Hecuba's revenge against Polymestor, in Euripides's
tragedy and – more starkly – in Ovid's *Metamorphoses*, turns her
from a noble, proud and grieving woman into a dog with fiery
eyes thirsting for blood.[7] Such images of female avengers – rare
as they are – are replicated in Renaissance revenge tragedies. In
Shakespeare's *Titus Andronicus* Tamora, the Queen of the Goths,
is thrust into the role of revenger when Titus refuses to heed her
pleas to spare the life of her son. Here there is no metamorphosis: there is no passage, as there is with Titus, from grief and

117

suffering to revenge, and consequently the play invites no sympathetic engagement with her position. She pleads with Titus to show qualities of mercy and pity that she does not herself possess. At the first opportunity she instructs her two surviving sons to demonstrate their filial love by revenging themselves on Bassianus and Lavinia. As her sons prepare to rape and mutilate Lavinia, Tamora's incitement to revenge is presented, through Lavinia's unheeded appeals, as the antithesis of the feminine: 'No grace? No womanhood? Ah, beastly creature,/ The blot and enemy to our general name!/ Confusion fall –' (II. ii. 182–4). In 'confusion', the penultimate word that Lavinia will ever speak, is communicated the unnaturalness of Tamora in urging such a revenge as that of sexual violation.

Francis Bacon in his essay 'On Revenge' had compared vengeful individuals to the malevolence of witches and such an analogy of the revenger and a transgressive female is revealing. Within social communities both witch and revenger are, or become, liminal subjects and when a woman takes on the role of the latter, she assumes the qualities of the former. When women do show a male resolve or become surrogate men, they are represented as out of control and deviant. The female avenger was generally seen as an aberration, a symbol of a world turned upside down, and, as such, demonized. The energies of female revenge were unnatural, depicted as more anarchic and more vociferously condemned than those of the male counterpart. In Ford's 'Tis Pity She's a Whore there are several revenge plots orchestrated by the male characters besides that of Hippolita, the abandoned lover of Soranzo. Her vengeance on Soranzo, she declares, will sweeten what her griefs have tasted and her plot follows dramatic precedence in taking place under cover of a masque performed at the wedding banquet of Annabella and Soranzo. Strikingly and symbolically, Hippolita enters dressed in white and crowned with a garland of willow. But her plot backfires as the poisoned cup of wine intended for Soranzo is given to her by the scheming Vasques. When her stratagem is revealed, the double standards inherent in revenge are ironically exposed in the response of the spectators. Vasques, who has no compunction about torturing and blinding Annabella's nurse Putana, condemns Hippolita and sees some kind of poetic justice in the way revenge has rebounded upon her: 'Foolish woman, thou art now like a firebrand, that hath kindled others and burnt thyself' (IV. i. 71–2). The guests at the banquet celebrate the 'wonderful justice' that has foiled Hippolita's plans, while in a final, defiant speech, recognizing her own damnation, all that Hippolita can now do in revenge is to curse the marriage of Soranzo and Annabella. That Hippolita's plot has brought to light Soranzo's duplicitous past seems lost on the wedding guests as they condemn her unequivocally as vile, lustful and proud. In her abortive revenge against Soranzo, a man who has used her and broken his promises to her, there is no suggestion that Hippolita might have some grievance against him. Preoccupied as she is, we might still expect Annabella to make some comment on the revelations about her husband, but she too can only allude to Hippolita's destructiveness turned back upon herself as a 'fearful sight'.

One of the few plays to resist the image of the aberrant female avenger is curiously the earliest revenge play of the popular theatre, *The Spanish Tragedy*. Central to the play's intricate plot are the stratagems of Lorenzo and Balthazar to secure Bel-imperia as bride for Balthazar, a marriage which is seen as the basis of an alliance to secure peace between Spain and Portugal. Bel-imperia has her own agenda and she exploits her beauty and her powerful character, attributes suggested in her allegorical name, to gain her ends. She has already acted unconventionally in taking Don Andrea – a man of lower social station – as a lover and, following his death in battle, plans a relationship with Horatio, a man of the same social caste as Don Andrea. Her motives are not entirely clear and this is reflected in her wooing of Horatio, in which both love and revenge play a part:

> Yes, second love shall further my revenge.
> I'll love Horatio, my Andrea's friend,
> The more to spite the prince that wrought his end.
>
> (I. iv. 66–8)

At this stage in the drama, however, she transgresses no gender boundaries and accepts that as a woman her means to revenge are confined to the exploitation of her sexuality.

Bel-Imperia dares to woo a socially inferior man, and although Lorenzo and Balthazar have sustained no injury from Horatio, they are quick to talk of revenge. The notion that

Horatio must pay with his life for loving Bel-imperia is utterly arbitrary and there is no cause for the violence of Balthazar and Lorenzo beyond frustrated desire and slight. Bel-imperia is as determined to revenge the death of her second lover as she was her first, but this time she demands bodily reparation and she turns to Hieronimo as her accomplice. In a letter written in blood, she informs him of the blood guilt of Balthazar and Lorenzo. Yet Hieronimo distrusts the authenticity of the letter; his delay prompts Bel-imperia to urge him to action, swearing that if he neglects his duty to avenge Horatio, she herself will dispose of the murderers:

> Nor shall his death be unrevenged by me,
> Although I bear it out for fashion's sake:
> For here I swear, in sight of heaven and earth,
> Shouldst thou neglect the love thou shouldst retain,
> And give it over and devise no more,
> Myself should send their hateful souls to hell
> That wrought his downfall with extremest death.

(IV. i. 22–8)

Bel-imperia is far from the stereotype of the unruly female avenger as she coolly disguises her intentions 'for fashion's sake'. She retains her wits in a way that Hieronimo does not: her presence of mind is vital to him as he stage-manages the murders of Lorenzo and Balthazar during the performance of *Soliman and Perseda* in which, as Perseda, she murders Balthazar, aptly playing the part of the unwelcome suitor, Soliman. Her readiness to perpetrate revenge is signalled ironically in the exchange before the play within a play. Hieronimo comments, 'For what's a play without a woman in it?' and she replies pertinently: 'Little entreaty shall serve me, Hieronimo,/ For I must needs be employed in your play.' Bel-imperia, too, *needs* to avenge the death of Horatio and, like Hieronimo, is ready to surrender life when this desire has been satisfied.

Despite the machinations of her brother, Bel-imperia's position as niece to the king of Spain allows her a degree of autonomy denied to less socially advantaged but no less theatrically powerful women. In *The White Devil*, Vittoria Corombona recognizes that she can retaliate against her enemies only through the manipulation of language. During her arraignment Vittoria expresses her desire for vengeance but, despite her ability to confound her accusers, she knows that she is powerless against them, declaring woman's revenge is poor since it 'dwells but in the tongue'. Nonetheless, Vittoria's verbal revenge is effective in exposing the hypocrisy of her male detractors, vehemently denouncing Cardinal Monticelso as having 'ravished justice'. Her male detractors move to contain the threat and, in one last attempt at demonization, they are quick to present her as unnatural when they claim, 'She's turned Fury', meaning that she is possessed by the spirit of vengeance. In *The Duchess of Malfi*, Webster's other great tragedy, it could be said that it is again the female protagonist who gains through words alone a moral retaliation against her murderers. In entertaining no thoughts of revenge against her brothers, she offers a challenge to the predominantly male code of practice. Her final message to them – 'Go tell my brothers, when I am laid out,/ They then may feed in quiet' (IV. ii. 236–7) – denies them the satisfaction of the revenge they have so viciously pursued and resists any notion of further retribution. The Duchess does, as has been pointed out, exemplify a norm of stoic womanhood;[8] yet her opposition to any perpetuation of revenge is, in its instinctive rather than deliberative aspect, unconventional for both sexes in plays of revenge.

THE REVENGE OF BUSSY D'AMBOIS

The Revenge of Bussy D'Ambois by George Chapman is the sequel to *The Tragedy of Bussy D'Ambois* and it is a rare example of retribution spilling over from one play to another. In general, there is an inherent stability in the pattern of revenge which depicts reparation following an initial act of violation or perceived injury, but where the story begins and how much of the original act is represented or reported is the dramatist's choice. At the end of *The Tragedy of Bussy D'Ambois* the Count of Montsurry had tricked Bussy, a rising star at court, into a meeting with Tamyra, his wife and Bussy's lover, and, with hired assassins, had murdered Bussy. Set amidst the factional intrigue of near contemporaneous French politics, dominated by the aspirant figure of the Duke of Guise, the second part dramatizes the dilemma of Clermont D'Ambois, as he deliberates over avenging the death of his brother.

121

In a revenge play that is so rational in tone it is curious that Chapman retains the supernatural element of the Ghost. Bussy's Ghost is, however, essential to the plot: the ghost is reported in the first scene as having appeared to Clermont to incite him to revenge and is seen on stage in the final act urging him not to neglect a revenge that is synonymous with justice. The predicament of the protagonist in *The Revenge of Bussy D'Ambois* suggests a parallel with Hamlet's delay and his self-searching response to the command of his father's ghost. Unlike Hamlet's meditative soliloquies, however, that communicate a free-wheeling, restless intelligence and subjectivity, Clermont's speeches are much more static in their expression of the stoic values which characterize him. His friend and ally the Duke of Guise – who, ironically, has been involved with Bussy's murder – describes Clermont as 'this Senecal man' and alludes admiringly to his indifference to Fortune's vicissitudes: 'Come fair or foul, whatever chance can fall,/ Fixed in himself, he still is one to all' (IV. iv 45–6). Chapman thus introduces into the Renaissance revenge play the values advocated in the philosophy of Seneca, but implicitly rejected by the protagonists of Seneca's plays. Stoicism, with its doctrine of passive acceptance of misfortunes and ills was, of course, at variance with the violent reaction demanded of the avenger. In Clermont's stance there is a rational approach to revenge that makes Chapman's play quite distinctive.[9] Revenge, Christian belief and stoicism are rather uneasily reconciled in the words of Bussy's ratiocinative ghost when it appears to remind Clermont to perform the task. However man may try to control the will, the mind, the Ghost argues, must not reject action if that action is imitative of divine retribution. Finally the Ghost returns to the more familiar concept of corrupted human justice that can only be remedied by individual action:

> Away then, use the means thou hast to right
> The wrong I suffered. What corrupted law
> Leaves unperformed in kings do thou supply,
> And be above them all in dignity.

> (V. i. 96–9)

The reasonable tone of the Ghost's reproach for inaction is typical of a play in which the expression of philosophical belief has largely replaced the obsessive endeavour and spectacular effects we have come to expect from revenge tragedy.

What makes *The Revenge of Bussy D'Ambois* of particular interest here is the roles ascribed to women in the perpetration of revenge. It is the females of the play who offer the most concerted challenge to Clermont's stoicism and the passivity that entails. At the beginning of the play we learn that Charlotte, the sister of Bussy and Clermont, has made it a condition of her marriage to Baligny that he revenge Bussy's death. Baligny would seem initially to be the just man speaking out against the corruption of the world. Later it transpires that he is working against Clermont and the Duke of Guise in the service of the king, but none of this is evident in his opening speech, when he inveighs against the 'declining kingdom' that has effectively condoned Bussy's murder as a warning against adultery. When Renel presses him to be more active in righting the wrongs done to Bussy, Baligny tells him of the vow he has made to Charlotte, but this, he then says, has been superseded: Clermont has promised to challenge Montsurry to a duel, 'the noblest and most manly course' of revenge. There appears to be a striking contrast between this open, declared act and the intrigue of other avengers desperately pursuing thwarted justice or acting covertly in retaliation for personal slight. All the unruly passions of revenge in Chapman's play seem to be contained within legitimate social and cultural practice. Revenge is seen as part of an aristocratic code of conduct that – since no justice operates through the office of the king – fulfils a just and, unusually in revenge plays, a public purpose.

Bussy's sister and his lover are not, however, satisfied at what they interpret as a failure to take immediate and right action. Charlotte is impatient at Clermont's 'dull vow' and continues to demand – despite the injunction of the Ghost – that her husband do the deed; 'so past her sex she urges', Baligny confides to Renel, that he almost fears to see her without the visual proof, of bloodied face and hands, that he has killed Montsurry. The second scene of the play opens with Tamyra's soliloquy in which she impatiently acknowledges the constraints on women in matters of revenge; all that she can do is weep until the moment when revenge is triumphant. Although she cannot act, like Vittoria in *The White Devil* she can attack verbally,

denouncing her husband for torture and tyranny, provoking his
clichéd response that she is a 'Fury'. Male anxiety about
Charlotte's and Tamara's usurpation of revenge is conveyed in
glossing the women as 'manly', 'great-spleened' and 'brave
virago'.

When Montsurry refuses to respond to Clermont's challenge,
feelings of unappeased revenge are again expressed through
these 'manly' women. This is most keenly articulated in a scene
between Clermont and Charlotte that is set up as a rational
debate about the ethics of revenge. Charlotte accuses her brother
of being defective in 'ling'ring my dear brother's wreak' and
demands to know why he responded to a villain like Montsurry
by such an honourable strategy as sending him a challenge. The
implication is that, by its very nature, revenge is contrary to such
a social code of practice as the men want to uphold. Clermont is
set on what he sees as a virtuous course of action, demanding of
Charlotte 'Shall we revenge a villainy with a villainy' and
regretting that his brother's spirit has demanded this usurpation
of 'public laws'. As we have seen, Bussy himself answers this
apprehension by claiming that the corrupted law has left justice
undone. In the scene of brother and sister confrontation,
Clermont attempts to pacify Charlotte with the argument that
such a fiery demand for revenge as hers is unwomanly: instead,
in what seems almost comically patronizing, he advises pursuits
appropriate to her sex, such as attending to her clothes,
complexion and powdering of her hair (III. ii. 127–42). Faced
with such an inadequate and ineffectual response, it is
predictable that Charlotte should turn on her brother, wishing
she could assume a traditionally masculine role:

> I would once
> Strip off my shame with my attire and try
> If a poor woman, votist of revenge,
> Would not perform it with a precedent
> To all you bungling, foggy-spirited men.

(III. ii. 162–6)

Charlotte is deflected from such transgendering by reports of a
plot against Clermont, but evidently she does not abandon the
idea and, like earlier male avengers, she is driven to distraction
by the failure to exact retribution. Renel informs Baligny that

she is 'so wild, so mad/ She cannot live and this unwreaked sustain' and hints at Charlotte's future action by comparing her to Medea. As Clermont continues to hesitate, Charlotte devises her own plan. When she next appears she is disguised as her own male servant, presenting herself to Tamyra as nominated by Charlotte to kill Montsurry. In a play like *The Revenger's Tragedy*, such a disguise involving an alter ego would have been the occasion for ironic *double entendre* and black humour, but there is no irony in this scene as Charlotte's plan is soon aborted by the appearance of Bussy's ghost. The Ghost puts an end to the women's plot, with the injunction that it is Clermont who 'must author this just tragedy'. While the Ghost is as impatient as Charlotte for vengeance, it follows convention in its insistence that retribution must remain a male prerogative and cannot be usurped by a woman.

The Revenge of Bussy D'Ambois does invert male and female roles. As we have seen, women are described – ruefully – as 'manly' and, with male avengers incapacitated, women are anxious to fulfil that role. As Clermont prepares to kill Montsurry in the final scene, he invites Tamyra to participate in the vengeance by torturing her husband in the way that he had tortured her in *The Tragedy of Bussy D'Ambois*. Montsurry's reaction exposes the usual double standards: 'O, shame of women, whither art thou fled?' The hypocrisy does not escape Clermont, who asks him whether it would be any greater shame for Tamyra to replicate a cruelty that Montsurry has earlier inflicted on her. The thought that he might be defeated by a woman spurs Montsurry to fight Clermont; as he calls on all deceived men to join him and revenge themselves on this 'race of Furies', he expresses a fear of emasculation. Charlotte, impatiently watching the fight from the balcony above, sees the act of revenge as unnecessarily protracted and in one final moment of female intervention, she enters below – still in male attire – declaring that she will join the fight and bring it to a speedy and satisfactory conclusion. Speaking still as her own male servant, she reproaches Clermont with her comment that his sister would not have stood to have her brother's vengeance 'in single combat stick so in her fingers'. As Clermont defeats Montsurry, conventional gender roles are reinstated. Montsurry dies commanding his wife to spend the rest of her life in penitence. After confronting male procrastination with repeated calls for action, the three women – Tamyra, Charlotte and the Countess – declare their intention to withdraw from court life and enter a convent. Bussy's ghost, appearing at the beginning of the fifth act, had called on 'ignorant men' to reform their 'manless lives'. Throughout the play the diseased, corrupt state has been identified with a degenerate king and a nobility largely driven by self-serving goals. That women desire to usurp male roles is seen both as a consequence of male ineffectuality and as contributing to subsequent moral and social degeneration. Female energies are subversive in the challenge they issue to the stoicism that the play, through Clermont's suicide, endorses and they must be contained. Chapman allows his female characters a greater role in the pursuit of revenge, and these allegedly deviant energies are played out. The women's voluntary seclusion provides a closure implying that their dramatically significant lives are now over.

THE MAID'S TRAGEDY

The Maid's Tragedy, a collaborative work by Francis Beaumont and John Fletcher, is the only play of the period in which a woman avenges her own honour and – significantly – that of her male kin, who are unwilling to act personally. In the tone and narrative of the opening scenes of the play, however, there is little to suggest that this is a revenge tragedy. We are thrust into the celebration of a court wedding; the dialogue is relaxed and urbane as the courtiers prepare for the performance of the wedding masque. One discordant note is caused by the discovery that Amintor, the bridegroom, has deserted a former love, Aspatia, to marry Evadne, in a union which we gather has been arranged by the king.

The plot builds slowly towards a startling revelation on the couple's wedding night, prompted by Evadne's refusal to sleep with Amintor. At first the bewildered Amintor considers Evadne's unresponsiveness to be due to excessive female modesty; he conjectures that she may have sworn to her companions to keep her maidenhead. Evadne is incredulous at Amintor's naïve view of female sexuality and remarks sardonically: 'A maidenhead, Amintor, at my years?' The line challenges all the conventional assumptions about female chastity,[10] just as Evadne's later role as avenger transgresses notions of woman's passivity. Indeed, the two extremes of conduct would seem to be concomitant. On her wedding night Evadne responds coolly to Amintor's desperate questioning, such that his theatrical appeal to heaven's thunder seems hopelessly out of place in the pragmatic dialogue that she has initiated. Amintor's anger mounts and he determines that when he knows who the man is, he will 'cut his body into motes/ And scatter it before the northern wind' (II. i. 299–300). This resolve is instantly shaken when Evadne reveals that it is the king who is her lover. In *The Revenge of Bussy D'Ambois*, Clermont had declared that it would be impious to touch the sacred person of the king in revenge for the murder of Guise. This too is Amintor's position. Reflecting the dominant ideological position that a subject cannot take the life of the king, Amintor expresses his loyalty in absolute terms:

> O, thou hast nam'd a word that wipes away
> All thoughts revengeful; in that sacred name,
> 'The King' there lies a terror. What frail man
> Dares lift his hand against it? Let the gods
> Speak to him when they please; till when, let us
> Suffer, and wait.
>
> (II. i. 307–12)

The doctrine of passive obedience – even to a tyrant – is here transposed, and arguably diluted, into a domestic context. Interestingly, in Amintor's generalized appeal to the 'gods' here and elsewhere in the play, there is no biblical frame to the idea of patient earthly suffering, as there is in *The Atheist's Tragedy*. Instead, the emphasis falls on the divine right of kings and Amintor articulates the absolutist principles of the Jacobean regime. Amintor looks for the restitution of his honour, but finds himself hamstrung by notions of royal sacrosanctity. When, after prurient questioning in public about their wedding night, the king orders Evadne and Amintor into his private presence, Amintor can no longer contain his anger, accusing the king of tyranny and threatening his life. He behaves like an affronted lover: the king has abused his bed and only the king's death, together with a public proclamation of his wrongs, will satisfy

Amintor. Yet, when the king reminds him of his own inviolability, Amintor represses his violent feelings, acknowledging again the king's divinity that must quell his rage. Caught between an unquestioned belief that his 'treacherous hand' cannot 'touch holy things' (III. i. 249–50) and bitterness at his own abject position, Amintor can only resort to angry denunciation of Evadne and to the expression of remorse for his treatment of Aspatia. Between what Amintor would like to do – avenge his honour – and what he knows he must do – accept his role and bow to the will of the king – there is no debate.

Sexual relations in the play are exploitative. The king has arranged the marriage to provide respectable cover for his liaison and takes his pleasure from Evadne when he will; Evadne tells the king that she would forsake him if he should be thrown 'from this height' (III. i. 172). Other relationships, particularly male friendship, such as that between Evadne's brother Melantius and Amintor, are more idealized. When Melantius, detecting his friend's unhappiness, teases out the situation from Amintor, his initial response is one of disbelief and anger that Amintor should have stigmatized his sister. Yet, in a play that is notable for abrupt changes of response, Melantius's intentions of redeeming Evadne's honour are soon displaced by the desire to kill the king and avenge Amintor. Enraged, he envisages the fate of the king – 'From his iron den I'll waken Death/ And hurl him on this King' (III. ii. 189–90) – claiming that he will not rest until Amintor's heart is at peace. The question of whether they should jointly take action against the king is neatly side-stepped by Amintor's reiterated, if reluctant, belief in royal inviolability: 'I dare not do a sin/ Or else I would. Be speedy' (III. ii. 227–8). Moments later, however, Amintor typically contradicts himself and warns Melantius against regicide. There is no suggestion that Melantius subscribes to this same ideology of passive obedience. When Amintor fears that a curse will follow Melantius for killing the king, Melantius replies obliquely that he will do what 'worth' – virtue – bids him do, 'and no more'. Nonetheless, although he is apparently free of Amintor's inhibitions, Melantius is keen to safeguard his position as he calculates the surest way of avenging his family's and his friend's honour and, in an inversion of sexual roles, incites Evadne to murder the king. The dynamics of the scene of confrontation between Melantius and his sister are pivotal to the play. Initially, Evadne scornfully defies her brother's attempts to shame her, at least until he threatens her with physical violence and public defamation. Evadne's changes in attitude from insolence to penitence, and then to resolving on regicide, occur within moments and we are given no psychological insight as to how they occur. Similarly, how Melantius comes to propose that Evadne do a deed from which Amintor has shied away is hardly understood. At first, Melantius conveys his sense of the conventional and limited female role in vengeance, commanding Evadne to curse the king, 'till the gods hear and deliver him/ To thy just wishes'. Then the idea of Evadne's killing the king erupts, apparently from nowhere, resolving the dilemma posed by Amintor. Honour can be restored without imperilling male bodies or souls.

Evadne's initial response to Melantius's call to regicide, that 'all the gods forbid it!' (IV. i. 144), is again swept aside without any apparent qualm, and she displays a resolution and a logic that is rare even amongst male avengers. Her rationale is a simple one: the king has destroyed her honour and she will repay by destroying him.[11] Yet there is an implicit recognition that such a deed goes against her sex and demands not just transgendering, as we have seen in *The Revenge of Bussy D'Ambois*, but de-sexing. Faced with the image of his lover holding a knife and threatening his life, the king calls her name and Evadne in reply denies her identity and disclaims her sex:

> I am not she, nor bear I in this breast
> So much cold spirit to be called a woman:
> I am a tiger; I am any thing
> That knows not pity.

> (V. i. 65–8)

Implicitly, in the imagery of transmogrification, Evadne accepts that murder and revenge are not a woman's business, and this idea is reiterated in the incredulous response of the male courtiers when they discover the regicide. In reply to one of the gentlemen of the chamber who reports on 'her woeful act', Cleon reiterates the feminine pronoun: 'Her act! A woman' (V. i.

131). Another gentleman, Strato, tries to deny female agency, insisting that Evadne was only 'an instrument' in the plot. Ironically, in his desperate appeals to Evadne, the king enlists conventional notions of feminine gentleness, sweetness and pity, none of which he has cause to believe are embodied in his sometime lover.

Evadne herself displays a dual sensibility. She is aware that the murder of the king goes against female norms of conduct and mentality, but she also sees her action as in some way recuperating not only her own honour, but all lost female honour. As she swears to her brother that she will do the deed, she calls on 'spirits of abused ladies' (IV. i. 169) to help in her performance. It is possible to read Melantius's reply, 'Enough', as betraying male anxiety that his sister is contradicting the spirit of this act of revenge in appropriating it in the cause of expressly female wrong. Certainly, Melantius sees Evadne's action as a restoration of Amintor's and of family honour rather than Evadne's own honour, which is irretrievable; he refers later to 'that never-cured dishonour of my sister'. Another double standard, in this instance relating to male honour, or reputation, and female honour, or chastity, is transparent. Yet Evadne rejects this notion of lost female honour. As she administers the fatal stab to the king, forgetting her earlier de-sexing, she reclaims retribution in feminine terms: 'this stroke/ For the most wronged of women!' (Fig. 11). In feminist terms this is an heroic moment, as Evadne recognizes her own exploitation and abasement and kills a man who has repeatedly been denounced as a tyrant but against whom no one but a woman has dared act.

The tragic maid of the play's title is not, however, Evadne but Aspatia, who is judged by the male characters as infinitely more 'wronged' than Evadne. In the earlier scenes of the play, Aspatia laments her desertion in lengthy speeches addressed to other women of the court. When she can bear her situation no longer, she plans her suicide by passing herself off as her brother and provoking Amintor to fight with her. The remorse Amintor feels over his treatment of Aspatia, prompting his suicide, contrasts with the horror with which he regards Evadne when she finally appears before him, blood-stained and carrying the knife. Evadne expects commendation and acceptance as his wife, but Amintor can only, fearfully, condemn her for an act he describes

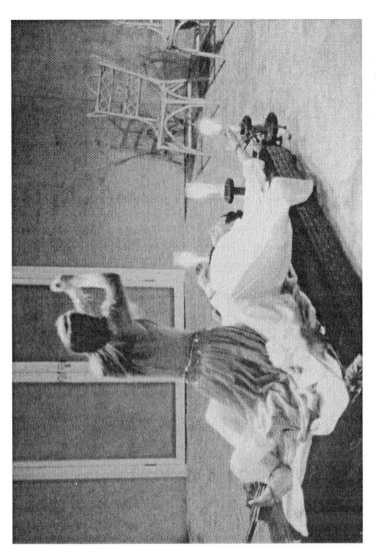

Figure 11. Sinéad Cusack as Evadne and John Carlisle as the King in the 1980 Royal Shakespeare Theatre production of *The Maid's Tragedy*, directed by Barry Kyle. Joe Cocks Studio Collection ©, Shakespeare Birthplace Trust.

as surpassing all her other faults. A tyrant king has been destroyed; this is an act that Amintor had earlier devoutly wished for, but this desire seems to be forgotten in his absolute abhorrence of Evadne's deed. Her subsequent suicide may mimic the archetypal fate of violated women, but it is represented not as heroic self-sacrifice, but as a desperate act of expiation. Such a gloss on her death is, of course, in accordance with her role as a sexually knowing woman rather than that of a chaste victim. For the men who have both incited the act and gained power from it, her suicide conveniently settles the fate of the female who has transgressed boundaries of sex and of subject.

The Maid's Tragedy is an appropriate play on which to conclude a study that has emphasized the individual distinctiveness of revenge plays of the English Renaissance. This is not only because it stands out for its projection – and rejection – of the female avenger, but also because it presents revenge as the matrix for other dramatic concerns. There is no central protagonist with a moral and psychological compulsion to revenge, and no protracted plotting to enable such a character to gain access to his enemy. The motives of revenge are muddied. It is seemingly dictated by honour, and yet Amintor at one point claims that honour in itself is nothing (IV. ii. 319), while Melantius believes that his sister's honour is irretrievable. By extension, revenge becomes an act devoid of meaning, arguably the occasion for men to plot against other men to advance their material interests. In terms of spectacle, the murder of the king does provide the sensational finale that characterizes most of the plays discussed in this study, but without cathartic effect. The king's sexual exploitation of a not unwilling woman is hardly the equivalent of the miscarriages of justice witnessed in earlier plays. Indeed, *The Maid's Tragedy* reveals the generic flexibility of revenge tragedy in that the tragedy is not that of the revenger, but is that of a subsidiary character. Aspatia's story has little to do with revenge and indeed she is valorized by being the antithesis of the female avenger.

This book began with a discussion of the essentialism of revenge and hence its perennial appeal as theatre. Audiences enjoy fantasies of violence and if the violence can be construed as just, pleasure in shocking entertainment can be rationalized. The paradigm of the wronged hero suffering stoically and enduring a period of restraint before he takes his revenge, enables the spectator to enjoy vicariously both the moral dilemma of the avenger and the spectacle of a 'just' murder. Such fictive explorations of vengeance are cathartic, as they cleanse but also warn against violence. Revenge plays reveal and acknowledge the human capacity for acts of savagery and counteractive violence and hence they release the spectator from the burden of repression. This is the primal appeal of a number of the plays discussed in this study. Yet, whatever the fundamental appeal of this drive for compensation, revenge tragedies of the Renaissance are culturally constructed. The plays we have examined, in their inherent notions of class, nationality and gender, exhibit artistically the ideologies of the English Renaissance. Equally, we can see how playwrights drew upon diverse facets of contemporary cultural and social life, from the pull of the mythologic to the manipulation of images of institutionalized punishment. Such conscious and unconscious assimilation of material produced revenge plays of remarkable range and, clearly, to see them from the premise of Elizabethan and Jacobean attitudes to revenge is seriously to confine them. Renaissance revenge plays are artistic constructs, and as such, they are inter-dependent, but also independent as the essentialism of revenge enters a unique fictional world.

Notes

INTRODUCTION: REVENGE AND REVENGE TRAGEDY

1. See 'On Anger', in Michel de Montaigne, *The Complete Essays*, trans. M. A. Screech (London, 1991), 809–16 (p. 816).
2. See *Seneca: Moral Essays*, trans. John W. Basore (London, 1928), 107–355.
3. Francis Bacon, 'On Revenge', *The Essays*, ed. John Pitcher (Harmondsworth, 1985), 73.
4. John Norden, *The Mirror of Honour* (1597), 24.
5. See, for example, Lily B. Campbell, 'Theories of Revenge in Renaissance England', *Modern Philology*, 38 (1931), 281–96; Eleanor Prosser, *Hamlet and Revenge* (Stanford, CA, 1971); R. Broude, 'Revenge and Revenge Tragedy in Renaissance England', *Renaissance Quarterly*, 28 (1975), 38–58; Roland Mushat Frye, *The Renaissance Hamlet* (Princeton, 1984), 22–37.
6. See 'The Arraignment and Confession of the Lord Sanquire for Murder', in *A Complete Collection of State Trials from the Earliest Period to the Year 1783*, ed. T. B. Howell (London, 1816), vol. 2, pp. 743–64.
7. See the Arden edition of *Titus Andronicus*, ed. Jonathan Bate (London, 1995), 79–80.
8. See Michel Foucault, *Discipline and Punish*, trans. Alan Sheridan (London, 1977), 9–45.
9. Tom Stoppard, *Rosencrantz and Guildenstern are Dead* (London, 1967), 57.
10. See Janet Clare, *Drama of the English Republic, 1649–1660* (Manchester, 2002), 18–21, and John Kerrigan, 'Revenge Tragedy Revisited: Politics, Providence and Drama, 1649–83', *Seventeenth Century*, 12:2 (1997), 207–29.
11. For a detailed exploration of comic revenge, see Linda Anderson, *A Kind of Wild Justice: Revenge in Shakespeare's Comedies* (Newark, DE, 1987).
12. John Kerrigan, *Revenge Tragedy: Aeschylus to Armageddon* (Oxford, 1996), 216.

134

13. The pioneering article is by Ashley H. Thorndike, 'The Relations of *Hamlet* to Contemporary Revenge Plays', *PMLA*, 17:2 (1902), 125–220.
14. Fredson Bowers, *Elizabethan Revenge Tragedy 1587–1642* (Princeton, 1940).
15. Charles A. Hallett and Elaine S. Hallett, *The Revenger's Madness: A Study of Revenge Tragedy Motifs* (Lincoln, NE, 1980).
16. See *Four Revenge Tragedies*, ed. Katherine Eisaman Maus (Oxford, 1995), ix–xxxi (p. ix).

CHAPTER 1. REVENGE AND JUSTICE: ELIZABETHAN REVENGE TRAGEDIES

1. See Arthur Freeman, *Thomas Kyd: Facts and Problems* (Oxford, 1967), 1–48.
2. See C. L. Barber, *Creating Elizabethan Tragedy: The Theater of Marlowe and Kyd*, edited, with an introduction, by Richard P. Wheeler (Chicago and London, 1988).
3. *Seneca His Tenne Tragedies* (London, 1581). The ninth tragedy, *Octavia*, is now known not to be by Seneca.
4. See *Jasper Heywood and his Translations of Seneca's Troas, Thyestes and Hercules Furens*, ed. H. De Vocht (Louvain, 1913), 191–5.
5. See Robert S. Miola, *Shakespeare and Classical Tragedy: The Influence of Seneca* (Oxford, 1992).
6. See G. C. Moore Smith, *Plays Performed in Cambridge Colleges before 1585*, in *Fasciculus Joanni Willis Clark dicatus* (London, 1909), 265–73.
7. Usually known as Procne. See Ovid, *Metamorphoses*, trans. Frank Justus Miller (London, 1916) 2 vols, 1, 289–339.
8. See W. Y. Durand, '*Palaemon and Arcyte, Progne, Marcus Geminus* and the theatre in which they were acted, as described by John Bereblock (1566)', *PMLA*, 20 (1905), 502–28 (pp. 515–16).
9. See Lukas Erne, *Beyond The Spanish Tragedy: A Study of the Works of Thomas Kyd* (Manchester, 2001), 95.
10. Richard Braithwait, *The English Gentlewoman* (1631), 54–5. The anecdote was repeated by William Prynne in his massive anti-theatrical work, *Histrio-mastix* (1633).
11. See *Henslowe's Diary*, ed. R. A. Foakes (Cambridge, 2nd edn, 2002).
12. For a review of the production, see Richard Proudfoot, 'Kyd's *Spanish Tragedy*', *Critical Quarterly*, 25:1 (1983), 71–6.
13. See Molly Smith, *Breaking Boundaries: Politics and Play in the Drama of Shakespeare and his Contemporaries* (Aldershot, 1998), 26–33.
14. *Titus Andronicus*, ed. Jonathan Bate (London, 1995), 6. See also

Heather James, 'Cultural Disintegration in *Titus Andronicus*: Mutilating Titus, Vergil, and Rome', *Themes in Drama: Violence in Drama*, 5:13 (1991), 123–40.

15. For reviews of Peter Brook's 1955 Stratford production, see Richard David, 'Drams of Eale', *Shakespeare Survey*, 10 (1957), 126–34, and Brook, '*Titus Andronicus*', *World Theatre*, 7 (1958), 27–9.

16. See 'Mourning and Melancholia', in *The Pelican Freud Library*, vol. 11, ed. Angela Richards (Harmondsworth, 1984), 251–68.

17. See Eugene Waith, 'The Metamorphosis of Violence in *Titus Andronicus*', *Shakespeare Survey*, 10 (1957), 39–49.

18. The critical commentary on *Hamlet* is so extensive that a selective bibliography would be impossible. For stimulating and controversial accounts of the Ghost, see G. Wilson Knight, 'The Embassy of Death: An Essay on *Hamlet*', in *The Wheel of Fire* (Oxford, 1930; repr. London, 1961), 17–47, and Stephen Greenblatt, *Hamlet in Purgatory* (Princeton, 2002), 151ff.

19. See, for example, Harold Bloom, *Shakespeare: The Invention of the Human* (London, 1999), 383–432.

20. See Barbara Everett, *Young Hamlet: Essays on Shakespeare's Tragedies* (Oxford, 1989), 11–36, 124–37.

21. See Romana Beyenburg, '*Hamlet*', in Pamela Mason and Keith Parsons (eds), *Shakespeare in Performance* (London, 1995), 67–74.

22. See John Kerrigan, *Revenge Tragedy* (Oxford, 1996), 188. See also Michael Neill, *Issues of Death: Mortality and Identity in English Renaissance Tragedy* (Oxford, 1997), 251–61.

23. See Harold Jenkins, *The Life and Work of Henry Chettle* (London, 1934), 71–3.

CHAPTER 2. REVENGE AND METATHEATRICALITY

1. See Philip J. Finkelpearl, *John Marston of the Middle Temple: An Elizabethan Dramatist in His Social Setting* (Cambridge, MA, 1969), 83–124.

2. See W. Reavley Gair, *The Children of Paul's: The Story of a Theatre Company, 1553–1608* (Cambridge, 1982).

3. See Finkelpearl, *John Marston*, 270.

4. See Rick Bowers, 'John Marston at the "Mart of Woe": The *Antonio* Plays', in T. F. Wharton (ed.), *The Drama of John Marston*, (Cambridge, 2000), 14–27.

5. The stage has been estimated at being twenty feet in width with a projection of ten feet. The hall would have held between fifty and a hundred spectators. See Gair, *The Children of Paul's*, 61–72.

6. See R. A. Foakes, 'John Marston's Fantastical Plays: *Antonio and Mellida*

and *Antonio's Revenge'*, *Philological Quarterly*, 41 (1962), 229–39.

7. See Thomas Lodge, *Wit's Misery* (1596), in *The Complete Works of Thomas Lodge*, ed. Edmund Gosse, 4 vols (Glasgow, 1883), vol. 4, p. 62.
8. See Bowers, 'John Marston at the "Mart of Woe"', 23.
9. See Mark Thornton Burnett, '"I will not swell like a tragedian": Marston's *Antonio's Revenge* in Performance', *Neuphilologische Mitteilungen*, 90 (1989), 311–20.
10. See, for example, David Lake, *The Canon of Thomas Middleton's Plays: Internal Evidence for the Major Problems of Dramatic Authorship* (Cambridge, 1979), and Jackson P. MacDonald, *Studies in Attribution: Middleton and Shakespeare* (Salzburg, 1979).
11. See Rowland Wymer, 'Jacobean Tragedy', in Michael Hattaway (ed.), *A Companion to English Renaissance Literature and Culture* (Oxford, 2000), 545–55 (p. 551).
12. See Scott McMillan, 'Acting and Violence: *The Revenger's Tragedy* and its Departures from *Hamlet*', *SEL*, 24 (1984), 275–91.
13. See 'The Ego and the Id and Other Works' in *The Standard Edition of the Complete Psychological Works of Sigmund Freud*, vol. 19 (London, 1961), 73–5.
14. See Jonathan Dollimore, *Radical Tragedy: Religion, Ideology and Power in the Drama of Shakespeare and his Contemporaries* (Brighton, 1984), 140.
15. See L. G. Salingar, '*The Revenger's Tragedy* and the Morality Tradition', in Ralph J. Kaufmann (ed.), *Elizabethan Drama: Modern Essays in Criticism* (New York, 1961), 208–25.
16. See Michael Billington, *Guardian*, 12 September 1987.

CHAPTER 3. THEATRE OF GOD'S JUDGEMENT

1. See R. A. Foakes, *Marston and Tourneur* (Harlow, 1978).
2. For an examination of the conceptions of 'Nature' in the Renaissance, see J. F. Danby, *Shakespeare's Doctrine of Nature: A Study of King Lear* (London, 1948), 15–53.
3. For a discussion of how this relates to stagecraft, see Huston Diehl, ' "Reduce Thy Understanding to Thine Eye": Seeing and Interpreting in *The Atheist's Tragedy*', *Studies in Philology*, 78 (1981), 47–60.
4. The play was produced at the Belgrade Theatre, Coventry, in 1979 and at the Birmingham Rep in 1994. Michael Coveney, commenting on the latter production, referred to the play's 'idiosyncratic vitality' (*Observer*, 27 February 1994).
5. *The Theatre of God's Judgements* (1597), 147–8.
6. *Radical Tragedy: Religion, Ideology and Power in the Drama of Shakespeare and his Contemporaries* (Brighton, 1984), 89.

7. See C. Ricks, 'The Moral and Political Structure of *The Changeling*', *Essays in Criticism*, 10 (1960), 290–306.
8. See William Empson, *Some Versions of the Pastoral* (1935), 44ff.

CHAPTER 4. REVENGE OUT OF ITALY

1. See Ann Rosalind Jones, 'Italians and Others: *The White Devil* (1612)', in David Scott Kastan and Peter Stallybrass (ed.), *Staging the Renaissance: Reinterpretations of Elizabethan and Jacobean Drama* (New York and London, 1991), 251–62.
2. For a general discussion of Italy as location in the drama, see Michele Marrapodi, A. J. Hoenselaars, Marcello Cappuzzo and L. Falzon Santucci (eds), *Shakespeare's Italy: Functions of Italian Locations in Renaissance Drama* (Manchester, 1997), 1–13.
3. Thomas Nashe, *The Unfortunate Traveller*, in *An Anthology of Elizabethan Prose Fiction*, ed. Paul Salzman, 205–311 (pp. 283–4).
4. See G. K. Hunter, 'English Folly and Italian Vice', in *Dramatic Identities and Cultural Tradition: Studies in Shakespeare and his Contemporaries* (Liverpool, 1978), 103–33.
5. There were, of course, variations on the representation of Italy in the period. See Manfred Pfister, 'Shakespeare and Italy, or the Law of Diminishing Returns', in Marrapodi *et al.* (eds), *Shakespeare's Italy*, 295–305.
6. Richard Braithwait, *The English Gentlewoman* (1631), 35.
7. Fynes Moryson, *Unpublished Chapters of Fynes Moryson's Itinerary: Being a Survey of the Conditions of Europe at the End of the Sixteenth-Century* (London, 1903), 157.
8. See 'The Arraignment and Confession of the Lord Sanquire for Murder', in, ed. T. B. Howell, *A Complete Collection of State Trials from the Earliest Period to the Year 1783* (London, 1816), vol. 2, p. 751.
9. Moryson, *Unpublished Chapters*, 160.
10. See the address 'To the Reader' prefacing the play.
11. See *The White Devil*, ed. John Russell Brown, pp. xxvi–xxvii.
12. See Lisa Jardine, *Still Harping on Daughters: Women and Drama in the Age of Shakespeare* (Brighton, 1983), 68–93.
13. This has been a recurrent theme in criticism on the play. See Elizabeth M. Brennan, 'The Relationship between Brother and Sister in the Plays of John Webster', *MLR*, 58 (1963), 488–94; William Empson, 'Mine Eyes Dazzle', *Essays in Criticism*, 14 (1964), 80–86; Bob Hodge, ' "Mine Eyes Dazzle": False Consciousness in Webster's Plays', in David Aers, Bob Hodge and Gunther Kress, *Literature, Language and Society in England, 1580–1680* (Totowa, NJ, 1981), 100–121.

14. See Freud, 'Mourning and Melancholia' in *The Pelican Freud Library*, vol. 11, 245–69 (p. 260).
15. See Paul Yachnin, *Stage-Wrights: Shakespeare, Jonson, Middleton and the Making of Theatrical Culture* (Pennsylvania, 1997), 98.
16. See Pina Marzi Ciotti, 'Bianca Cappello' in *The Medici Women* (Florence, 1996), 43–56.
17. See Inga-Stina Ewbank, 'Realism and Morality in *Women Beware Women*', in R. V. Holdsworth (ed.), *Three Jacobean Revenge Tragedies* (London, 1990), 196–207.
18. See Rowland Wymer, *Webster and Ford* (London, 1995), 91–2, and Julie Sanders, *Caroline Drama: The Plays of Massinger, Ford, Shirley and Brome* (Plymouth, 1999), 6.

CHAPTER 5. THE WOMAN'S PART

1. 'And yet to be revenged of a woman were a thing than love itself more womanish.' See John Lyly, *Endymion*, IV. iii. 130–31.
2. See the comments of Jonathan Dollimore, *Radical Tragedy*, 141–2.
3. The role of women in Renaissance tragedy is similar to that of women in classical tragedy. See Anne Pippin Burnett, *Revenge in Attic and Later Tragedy* (Berkeley, 1998), 142–76.
4. Richard Braithwait, *The English Gentlewoman*, 34–5.
5. See Alison Findlay, *A Feminist Perspective on Renaissance Drama* (Oxford, 1999), 50.
6. See *The Eumenides* in Aeschylus, *The Oresteia*, trans. Robert Fagles (Harmondsworth, 1977).
7. There are a number of insightful readings of Hecuba as avenger. See Judith Mossman, *Wild Justice: A Study of Euripides' Hecuba* (Oxford, 1995); Burnett, pp. 157–76 and Martha Nussbaum, 'The Betrayal of Convention: a Reading of Euripides' *Hecuba*', chapter 13 in *The Fragility of Goodness: Luck and Ethics in Greek Tragedy and Philosophy* (Cambridge, 2001), 397–421.
8. See Dympna Callaghan, *Women and Gender in Renaissance Tragedy* (Hemel Hempstead, 1989), p. 151.
9. See Richard S. Ide, 'Exploiting the Tradition: The Elizabethan Revenger as Chapman's "Complete Man"', *Medieval and Renaissance Drama in England* (New York, 1984), I, 159–86.
10. See the discussion of *The Maid's Tragedy* by Kathleen McLuskie, in *Renaissance Dramatists* (Hemel Hempstead, 1989), 193–224.
11. See Eileen Allman, *Jacobean Revenge Tragedy and the Politics of Virtue* (Newark, 2000), pp. 129–46.

Select Bibliography

The bibliography excludes specific entries on Shakespeare's *Hamlet* and *Titus Andronicus*. Work on these plays in relation to revenge is cited in the notes to chapter 1. I have cited only the major twentieth-century editions of non-Shakespearean revenge plays.

EDITIONS

Francis Beaumont and John Fletcher

The Maid's Tragedy, ed. T. W. Craik (London, 1988).
The Maid's Tragedy, ed. Andrew Gurr (Edinburgh, 1969).
The Maid's Tragedy, ed. Howard B. Norland (Lincoln, NE, 1968).
The Maid's Tragedy, in *Four Jacobean Sex Tragedies*, ed. Martin Wiggins (Oxford, 1998).

Thomas Kyd

The Spanish Tragedy, ed. David Bevington (Manchester, 1996).
The First Part of Hieronimo and the Spanish Tragedy, ed. Andrew Cairncross (Lincoln, NE, 1967).
The Spanish Tragedy, ed. Philip Edwards (Manchester, 1988).
The Spanish Tragedy, in *Four Revenge Tragedies*, ed. Katherine Eisaman Maus (Oxford, 1995).
The Spanish Tragedy, ed. J. R. Mulryne (London and New York, 2nd edn, 1989).

George Chapman

The Revenge of Bussy D'Ambois, ed. Robert J. Lordi (Salzburg, 1977).
The Revenge of Bussy D'Ambois, in *Four Revenge Tragedies*, ed. Katherine

Eisaman Maus (Oxford, 1995).

Henry Chettle

The Tragedy of Hoffman, Malone Society Reprints, ed. Harold Jenkins (Oxford, 1951).
The Tragedy of Hoffman, ed. J. D. Jowett (Liverpool, 1983).

John Ford

'Tis Pity She's a Whore, ed. N. W. Bawcutt (London, 1966).
'Tis Pity She's a Whore, in *Selected Plays of John Ford*, ed. Colin Gibson (Cambridge, 1986).
'Tis Pity She's a Whore, ed. Lisa Hopkins (London, 2003).
'Tis Pity She's a Whore, in *'Tis Pity She's a Whore and Other Plays*, ed. Marion Lomax (Oxford, 1995).
'Tis Pity She's a Whore, ed. Brian Morris (London, 1968).
'Tis Pity She's a Whore, ed. Derek Roper (London, 1975).

John Marston

Antonio's Revenge, ed. Reavley Gair (Manchester, 1978).
Antonio's Revenge, ed. G. K. Hunter (London, 1966).

Thomas Middleton

The Revenger's Tragedy
The Revenger's Tragedy, in *Four Revenge Tragedies*, ed. Katherine Eisaman Maus (Oxford, 1995).
The Revenger's Tragedy, ed. R. A. Foakes (London, 1966).
The Revenger's Tragedy, ed. R. A. Foakes (Manchester, 1996).
The Revenger's Tragedy, ed. Lawrence J. Ross (Lincoln, 1966).

The Changeling
The Changeling, ed. N. W. Bawcutt (London, 1958; reprinted with additions, 1961).
The Changeling, ed. N. W. Bawcutt (Manchester, 1998).
The Changeling, ed. Joost Daalder (London, 1990).
The Changeling, in *Six Renaissance Tragedies*, ed. Colin Gibson (Basingstoke, 1997).
The Changeling, in *The Selected Plays of Thomas Middleton*, ed. David L. Frost (Cambridge, 1978).
The Changeling, ed. Patricia Thomson (London, 1964).

141

The Changeling, ed. George Walton Williams (London, 1967).

Women Beware Women
Women Beware Women, ed. Charles Barber (Edinburgh, 1969).
Women Beware Women, ed. William C. Carroll (London, 1968).
Women Beware Women, ed. Roma Gill (London, 1968).
Women Beware Women, ed. J. R. Mulryne (London, 1975).

Cyril Tourneur

The Atheist's Tragedy, ed. Roma Gill and Brian Morris (London, 1976).
The Atheist's Tragedy, in *Four Revenge Tragedies*, ed. Katherine Eisaman Maus (Oxford, 1995).
The Atheist's Tragedy, ed. Irving Ribner (Cambridge, MA, 1964).

John Webster

The Duchess of Malfi
The Duchess of Malfi, ed. Elizabeth Brennan (London, 1964).
The Duchess of Malfi, ed. John Russell Brown (London, 1964).
The Duchess of Malfi, ed. John Russell Brown (Manchester, 1997).
The Duchess of Malfi, ed. Brian Gibbons (London, 2001).
The Duchess of Malfi, ed. Kathleen McLuskie and Jennifer Uglow (Bristol, 1989).

The White Devil
The White Devil, ed. John Russell Brown (London, 1960).
The White Devil, ed. John Russell Brown (Manchester, 1996).
The White Devil (with *The Duchess of Malfi*), in *The Selected Plays of John Webster*, ed. Jonathan Dollimore and Alan Sinfield (Cambridge, 1983).
The White Devil, ed. Christina Luckyj (London, 1996).

CRITICISM

Francis Beaumont and John Fletcher

Broude, Ronald, 'Divine Right and Divine Retribution in Beaumont and Fletcher's *The Maid's Tragedy*', in W. R. Elton and William B. Long (eds), *Shakespeare and Dramatic Tradition* (1989).
McLuskie, Kathleen, *Renaissance Dramatists* (Hemel Hempstead, 1989), 193–224.
Shullenberger, William, '"This for the Most Wronged of Women": A

Reappraisal of *The Maid's Tragedy'*, *Renaissance Drama*, NS 13 (1982), 131–56.

Turner, Robert Y., 'Responses to Tyranny in John Fletcher's Plays', *Medieval and Renaissance Drama in England*, 4 (1989), 123–41.

Thomas Kyd

Barber, C. L., *Creating Elizabethan Tragedy: The Theater of Marlowe and Kyd* (Chicago and London, 1988).

Erne, Lukas, *Beyond the Spanish Tragedy: A Study of the Works of Thomas Kyd* (Manchester, 2001).

Shapiro, James, '"Tragedies naturally performed": Kyd's Representation of Violence: *The Spanish Tragedy*', in David Scott Kastan and Peter Stallybrass (eds), *Staging the Renaissance: Reinterpretations of Elizabethan and Jacobean Drama* (London, 1991).

Smith, Molly, *Breaking Boundaries: Politics and Play in the Drama of Shakespeare and his Contemporaries* (Aldershot, Hants, 1998).

George Chapman

Braunmuller, A. R., *Natural Fictions: George Chapman's Major Tragedies* (Delaware and London, 1990).

Ide, Richard S., 'Exploiting the Tradition: The Elizabethan Revenger and Chapman's "Complete Man"', *Medieval and Renaissance Drama in English*, 1 (1984), 159–86.

Henry Chettle

Glady, Sarah, J., 'Revenge as Double Standard in *The Tragedy of Hoffman*', *Discoveries*, 18:2 (2001).

Jenkins, Harold, *The Life and Work of Henry Chettle* (London, 1934).

John Ford

Champion, Larry S., 'Ford's *'Tis Pity She's a Whore* and the Jacobean Tragic Perspective', *PMLA*, 90 (1975), 78–87.

Farr, Dorothy M., *John Ford and the Caroline Theatre* (London, 1979).

Lomax, Marion, *Stage Images and Traditions: Shakespeare to Ford* (Cambridge, 1987).

Sanders, Julie, *Caroline Drama: The Plays of Massinger, Ford, Shirley and Brome* (Plymouth, 1999).

Wiseman, Susan J., *'Tis Pity She's a Whore: Representing the Incestuous Body'*, in Lucy Gent and Nigel Llewellyn (eds), *Renaissance Bodies: The Human Figure in English Culture c. 1540–1660* (London, 1990), 180–97.

Wymer, Rowland, *Webster and Ford* (London, 1995).

John Marston

Ayres, Philip J., 'Marston's *Antonio's Revenge*: The Morality of the Revenging Hero', *SEL*, 12 (1972), 359–74.

Baines, Barbara, J., '*Antonio's Revenge*: Marston's Play on Revenge Plays', *SEL*, 23 (1983), 277–94.

Bowers, Rick, 'John Marston at the "Mart of Woe": The *Antonio* Plays', in T. F. Wharton (ed.), *The Drama of John Marston* (Cambridge, 2000), 14–27.

Burnett, Mark Thornton, '"I will not swell like a tragedian": Marston's *Antonio's Revenge* in Performance', *Neuphilologische Mitteilungen*, 90 (1989), 311–20.

Finkelpearl, Philip J., *John Marston of the Middle Temple* (Cambridge, MA, 1969).

Foakes, R. A., 'John Marston's Fantastical Plays: *Antonio and Mellida* and *Antonio's Revenge*', *Philological Quarterly*, 41 (1962), 229–39.

Thomas Middleton

The Revenger's Tragedy

Coddon, Karin S., '"For show or useless property": Necrophilia and *The Revenger's Tragedy*', *English Literary History*, 61 (1994), 71–88.

Foakes, R.A., 'The Art of Cruelty: Hamlet and Vindici', *Shakespeare Survey* (1973), 21–32.

Salingar, L. G., '*The Revenger's Tragedy* and the Morality Tradition', repr. in R. V. Holdsworth (ed.), *Three Jacobean Revenge Tragedies* (London, 1990).

Simmons, J. L., 'The Tongue and its Office in *The Revenger's Tragedy*', *PMLA*, 92 (1977), 56–8.

Wymer, Rowland, 'Jacobean Tragedy', in Michael Hattaway (ed.), *A Companion to English Renaissance Literature and Culture* (Oxford, 2000), 545–55.

The Changeling

Empson, William, *Some Versions of the Pastoral* (London, 1935).

Malcolmson, C., '"As Tame as the Ladies": Politics and Gender in *The Changeling*', *ELR*, 20 (1990), 320–39.

Ricks, C., 'The Moral and Political Structure of *The Changeling*', *Essays in Criticism*, 10 (1960), 290–306.

Stachniewski, John, 'Calvinist Psychology in Middleton's Tragedies', in R. V. Holdsworth (ed.), *Three Jacobean Revenge Tragedies* (London, 1990), 226–47.

Women Beware Women

Bruzzi, Zara and A. A. Bromham, '"The soil alters; Y'are in another country": Multiple Perspectives and Political Resonances in Middleton's *Women Beware Women*', in Michele Marrapodi, A. J. Hoenselaars, Marcello Cappuzzo and L. Falzon Santucci (eds), *Shakespeare's Italy: Functions of Italian Locations in Renaissance Drama* (Manchester, 1997), 251–71.

Ewbank, Inga-Stina, 'Realism and Morality in *Women Beware Women*', in R. V. Holdsworth (ed.), *Three Jacobean Revenge Tragedies* (London, 1990), 196–207.

Foster, V. A., 'The Deed's Creature: The Tragedy of Bianca in *Women Beware Women*', *Journal of European and Germanic Philology*, 78 (1979), 508–21.

Heinemann, Margot, *Puritanism and Theatre: Thomas Middleton and Opposition Drama under the Early Stuarts* (Cambridge, 1980).

Schoenbaum, S., *Middleton's Tragedies: A Critical Study* (New York, 1955).

Cyril Tourneur

Diehl, Huston, 'Reduce Thy Understanding to Thine Eye: Seeing and Interpreting in *The Atheist's Tragedy*', *Studies in Philology*, 78 (1981), 47–60.

Ekeblad (Ewbank), Inga-Stina, 'An Approach to Tourneur's Imagery', *Modern Language Review*, 54 (1959), 489–98.

Foakes, R. A., *Marston and Tourneur* (Harlow, 1978).

Higgins, M. H., 'The Influence of Calvinistic Thought in Tourneur's *Atheist's Tragedy*', *Review of English Studies*, 19 (1943), 255–62.

Murray, P. B., *A Study of Cyril Tourneur* (Philadelphia, 1964).

Salingar, L. G., 'Tourneur and the Tragedy of Revenge', in Boris Ford (ed.), *The Age of Shakespeare* (Harmondsworth, 1982), 436–56.

John Webster

The Duchess of Malfi

Bradbrook, M. C., *John Webster: Citizen and Dramatist* (London, 1980).

Callaghan, Dympna (ed.), *The Duchess of Malfi*, New Casebooks (London, 2000).

Cave, Richard, *Text and Performance: 'The White Devil' and 'The Duchess of Malfi'* (London, 1988).

Ekeblad (Ewbank), Inga-Stina, 'The "Impure Art" of John Webster', *Review of English Studies*, 9 (1958), 253–67.

Forker, C. R., *The Skull Beneath the Skin: The Achievement of John Webster* (Illinois, 1986).

Jardine, Lisa, *Still Harping on Daughters: Women and Drama in the Age of*

Shakespeare (Brighton, 1983).

Pearson, Jacqueline, *Tragedy and Tragicomedy in the Plays of John Webster* (Manchester, 1980).

Wiggins, Martin, *Journeymen in Murder*: The Assassin in English Renaissance Drama (Oxford, 1991).

The White Devil

Boklund, Gunnar, *The Sources of The White Devil* (Cambridge, MA, 1957).

Bromley, Laura G., 'The Rhetoric of Feminine Identity in *The White Devil*', in Dorothea Kehler and Susan Baker (eds), *Another Country: Feminist Perspectives on Renaissance Drama* (Metuchen, NJ, 1991), 50–70.

Jones, Ann Rosalind, 'Italians and Others: *The White Devil*', in David Scott Kastan and Peter Stallybrass (eds), *Staging the Renaissance: Reinterpretations of Elizabethan and Jacobean Drama* (New York and London, 1991), 251–63.

Luckyj, Christina, *A Winter's Snake: Dramatic Form in the Tragedies of John Webster* (Athens, Georgia, 1989).

GENERAL CRITICISM

Allman, Eileen Jorge, *Jacobean Revenge Tragedy and the Politics of Virtue* (Cranbury, NJ, 1999).

Bowers, F. T., *Elizabethan Revenge Tragedy 1587–1642* (Princeton, 1940).

Braden, Gordon, *Renaissance Tragedy and the Senecan Tradition: Anger's Privilege* (New Haven, 1985).

Burnett, Anne Pippin, *Revenge in Attic and Later Tragedy* (Berkeley, 1998).

Hallett, Charles A. and Elaine S., *The Revenger's Madness: A Study of Revenge Tragedy Motifs* (Lincoln, 1980).

Hill, Eugene D., 'Revenge Tragedy', in Arthur F. Kinney (ed.), *A Companion to Renaissance Drama* (Oxford, 2002), 326–35.

Kerrigan, John, *Revenge Tragedy: Aeschylus to Armageddon* (Oxford, 1996).

Keyishian, Harry, *The Shapes of Revenge: Victimization, Vengeance and Vindictiveness in Shakespeare* (New Jersey, 1995).

Kiss, Attila, *The Semiotics of Revenge: Subjectivity and Abjection in English Renaissance Tragedy* (Szeged, 1995).

Mercer, Peter, *Hamlet and the Acting of Revenge* (London, 1987).

Watson, Robert, 'Tragedies of Revenge and Ambition', in Claire McEachern (ed.), *The Cambridge Companion to Shakespearean Tragedy* (Cambridge, 2002).

Wymer, Rowland, 'Jacobean Tragedy', in Michael Hattaway (ed.), *A Companion to Renaissance Literature and Culture* (Oxford, 2000), 545–55.

Index

147

Printed in the United Kingdom
by Lightning Source UK Ltd.
115850UKS00001B/168